FOOD & FOLKLIFE

All the Year Round in Southern Sweden

FOOD & FOLKLIFE

All the Year Round in Southern Sweden

ARENA

RECIPES:
Sam Hellhager

TEXT:
Anders Salomonsson
Leif Eriksson

ILLUSTRATIONS:
All food and other pictures not mentioned in the credits list on page 191 are by *Gunnar Magnusson, Magnusson Produktion AB*, Malmö

DESIGN AND PICTURE EDITING:
Nyebølle Grafisk Form AB, Helsingborg

RECIPE CHECKING:
Berit Selén, Home Economics teacher, Eskilstuna

LIST QUOTATIONS:
Folklivsarkivet, University of Lund

PROJECT GROUP:
Lena Engdahl, Lill Forsman
Bokbolaget AB, Malmö

TRANSLATION:
Roger Tanner,
Ordväxlingen AB, Hässelby

REPRO:
PrePress Center, Lund

PRINTING:
Fälth & Hässler, Värnamo 2002

BINDING:
Fälth & Hässler, Farsta 2002

PAPER, BOOK PAGES:
Silverblade matt 150 g

PAPER, DUST WRAPPER:
Galerie art gloss

TYPEFACES:
Janson text
Gill Sans

ISBN-nummer 91-7843-167-0

THANKS TO:
Folklivsarkivet, University of Lund, for quotations from lists and for illustrations.

Häckeberga Wärdshus, for letting us cook, taste and photograph the food.

Johan Törnquist and *Patrik Rambow*, who inspired Sam in his recipe writing.

Bo-Anders Dahlskog, Folklivsarkivet, University of Lund, for fascinating insights into the folk music of Skåne.

Höganäs Keramik, for lending us tableware.

Lennart Kjellgren, for lending us old Skåne song books.

Börje Larsson, for a vivid, smoked history of Skåne's culture.

Lars Lendrop, for guiding us behind the scene in the exciting ambience of Skåne's restaurants.

Kai Nyström, for the stories about foody trips to Denmark.

Vicky Offerlind, Offerlinds Spettkaksbageri, Genarp, for the sweetest tale in the book.

Åsa Ormell, Wallåkra Stenkärlsfabrik, for beautiful craftsmanship and inspiring company.

Vin- och Sprithistoriska Museet, for assistance in producing those wonderful schnapps labels.

Kjell Åkesson, for many fascinating touch-downs in the world of Malmö pub music.

Contents

Glimpses from "A Five-Day Journey in Skåne," 1795

"Skåne girls hay-making." Watercolour by Carl August Ehrensvärd

"The women's linen clothing is, as it were, a linen skirt with no lining sewn on to a linen blouse with no lining, so that during hay-making and corn harvesting the girls go about in this linen fabric as if in costume.

Fully apparelled, they wear short skirts with linen hems, they plait their hair with red and blue ribbons and over this sometimes wear a white rubbed cloth adorned with tassels, spread out and knotted, the wife's longer than the girl's."

"There is no sky more blissful than Skåne's, but the place that bears the food invariably repays with its own weight. Nothing but corn, cattle and sunshine in summer. Rain, wind and crows in autumn and drifts and ocean depths of snow in winter. In spring-time, thawed-out grannies among the tussocks. But I have never heard the farmer complain about it or wish to live in northern parts."

"From the highway, scattered sights are often beheld by reason of the country's customs and the season of the year.

Sometimes one may meet seven or eight well-dressed country women, all piled onto a single cart, returning from work at the manor in the company of many other flower-laden dung carts, always at the full trot. Never ill-dressed people on the road. The highway here is the peasant folk's gallery.

Sometimes you see the daughters of Strength deployed in clean linen on meadow and field, between armies of rosy-cheeked farmers.

Sometimes assembled for day works, adorned as if for a festival, not for labour.

Sometimes you see them at the church, when of course they are still more decorated.

Their daily working clothes always immaculately clean and neat."

Carl August Ehrensvärd
PAINTER AND PHILOSOPHER

17th century map of Skåne.

FOOD & FOLKLIFE

All the Year Round in Southern Sweden

This book is a sampler of Skåne's gastronomy, from early spring to infernal winter. It contains recipes for newly composed dishes, based on Scanian raw materials and culinary tradition, and a good deal of cultural history into the bargain.

Skåne has always been a transit land, a mingling point of impressions and influences from north and south. In addition, the food of Skåne has been more heavily spiced and salted than further north, both spices and salt being cheaper here than elsewhere: Skåne, then as now, was a first port of call for shipping from further south. So we have taken the liberty of decking our recipes with one or two imported ingredients.

The recipes have as far as possible been adapted to the modern kitchen and requirements of nutritional balance. Our motto: regional gastronomy in modern dress.

We sing the seasons, with all their changes and firstlings, festivals and customs, food and drink. Annual festivals and tradition are passed in review, explained and remarked on. Other topics include one or two Scanian hostelry interiors, pictures of life on board the old Copenhagen boats and descriptions of smoke-houses and pottery. These last mentioned were written by the author Leif Eriksson.

Be our guests!

Sam Hellhager   Anders Salomonsson

SPRING

Land that art blessed

Land that art blessed
carrot and celery
leek and potato
herring and schnapps.

These last mentioned delicacies
belong to a garden?
But of course, everything returns
to the soil
everything belongs to the ecocycle
Oh best beloved
wealth and tilth
earth and worth
the seeds that feed
us children and children
in ages upon ages and ages
your fork and your spade
all that ever you laid
in earth grows and stretches
to tilth and land
labour and laughter
butter and batter.

Winter and cold
and cracking of the earth
spring-earth-ding-ding
the sun with the seeds
the green shoots
in the rope of the winds.

New leaves in a row
with beetroot, dill and parsley
and annual weeds – chickweed
perennial – couch grass and
ground elder or younger
Oh best beloved.

The earth sweating against the
spade
kale and cabbage
onion and marrow
garlic and red onion
chive and swede
lettuce and black radish
herring and Skåne.

The sound in the ground
line after line
on the ground
Oh best beloved.

CARL MAGNUS VON SETH
From *"Land du välsignade"*, 1993

The Food of Spring

"*Spickeskinka*, *spickekorv* and *spickesill* – ham, sausage and herring respectively – get their names from the practice of using "spicks" (slivers of wood) to nail them up to dry (most often after salting and/ or smoking). Thus treated, the – usually – pork or sausage would keep for a long time. Some things might shrivel out of recognition, but they would not be spoiled, they could be soaked and then cooked in soup and broth without any loss of flavour or nutritional value. Ham and goose breast, on the other hand, came out of it all looking remarkably appetising.

An old saying had it that you were not to touch the *spickeskinka* (ham) before the cuckoo had been heard. That way it must have hung for something like six months, from the pre-Christmas slaughter until May. Parallels to this rule already existed on the continent in the 8th century. Why was this? The forty days of Lent may have played their part, but I think the real reason is something else. Spring was a season of short commons. Stocks of meat could only be filled up by slaughtering animals which had been on starvation diet all winter. People were reluctant to do this, and so the proceeds of the autumn butchering had to be saved as long as possible.

What else did people have to live on? Well, of course, they had what remained of the meat and herring they had salted down in barrels. A writer born in 1874 records, from the Vemmenhög area: "The diet was very plain, consisting mainly of pork and herring with potatoes. Boiled pork was usually eaten cold. It was only eaten warm with freshly boiled potatoes and mustard dip."

The old tale – if it was just a tale – about poor people with the approach of spring having to make do with dipping potato or a piece of crisp bread in the pickling liquid from the herring or pork is amply documented in our ethnographic archives. With the approach of spring, people – at any rate, those living near the coast – could eke out their salt herring with fresh fish. The lumpfish came into Öresund in March, and the ide swam up the rivers to spawn early on and was an easy prey.

After lambing in March, the sheep began to yield milk. All of it went to the lambs at first, but after a few weeks a careful start could be made to milking the ewes.

Another Vemmenhög reminiscence: "One very popular dish in my boyhood was *syltemjölk*. I still eat it [1931]. It's sheep's milk boiled soon after milking and then left to stand until it thickens, which gives it a sharp flavour. The milk would be in a dish in the middle of the table, and you would dip into it with a piece of bread on the point of a knife."

One way and other, sheep were of much greater economic importance in the old days than they are now. Perhaps mutton was cooked in a plainer fashion which, according to old descriptions, left it tasting of "woolly cardigan". But that was before the flavouring of joints of lamb developed into the fine art it is today.

Just as sheep's milk was a *primeur*, a firstling, people longed for the first draught of cow's milk. After the long "dry season" of winter, they longed for pancakes made with real milk, not just water, and perhaps they made green cheese and churned a little butter (instead of the green-salted dripping they had had to make do with during spring), though in the old agrarian economy milk was really a preserve and hard currency.

"A Farmer's Dwelling in Skåne." Watercolour by Nils Månsson Mandelgren, 1852.

Marking the eggs with the farm's name before selling them to the shop. Skurup, 1910s.

Dark rye bread (kavring) emerging from the oven. Torrlösa, 1950.

But spring wasn't all emptiness and poverty. One foodstuff after another reappeared for the new season. We have already mentioned eggs and milk, and to them were added potatoes, turnips, cabbage, onions and all manner of green vegetables. Those who were short of potatoes had to make do with turnips. Somebody from Häglinge recalls:

"When I was young we were hard up for potatoes, so we had to eat turnips instead. We used to sow turnips on a patch of rough ground which we broke up a bit with a hoe. They never came to much. In winter we would slice them and fry them in the baking oven after we'd been making bread. We'd fry about ten or twelve at a time."

Cabbage and root vegetables were staple food at the onset of spring. In some places there were firm rules for getting peas and root vegetables to prosper and multiply:

"All root vegetables and bulbous plants should be planted when the moon is on the wane, but all flowers at the full moon. You get good peas if you sow them on a Wednesday or Sunday during the final quarter of the moon. And it's a good idea to sow parsley at the same time, because

"The Kneading Trough."
Watercolour by Frans Lindberg.

then it turns out better," a Fru Alstad villager assures us.

Bread and porridge were also basic foods, especially in the south of Skåne, where grain growing was more important than further north in the province, and above all people relied on rye bread made with yeast. If it was made from screened flour it was called fine bread, otherwise it was coarse. In a book on the food and customs of Skåne, published in 1934, Nanna Lundh-Eriksson tells us that you get the kind of rye bread called kavring "if you put the loaves on top of each other in a moderate oven, leave them there for ten or twelve hours and then separate them to finish baking."

Shrovetide, Lent and Easter

Chronologically speaking, some people find Easter an unruly festival, coming as it does sometimes in March, sometimes in April. The reason for this variation is to be found in ecclesiastical decision made during the infancy of Christianity. We needn't go into that now. Suffice it to say that Easter Day comes on the first Sunday after the first full moon after 20th March. So it is the phases of the moon that decide, with the result that Easter can vary by a whole month, from 21st March onwards.

First, though, we have Lent, and before that we have Shrovetide, though not everyone nowadays is quite clear about this. *Shrovetide* begins with Shrove Sunday (Quinquagesima) and lasts for three days, ending with Shrove Tuesday. This meant that people had three days to eat their fill and enjoy themselves in various ways before the forty days of fasting which followed. In Skåne in olden times, this Sunday was called "Pork Sunday" and the day after "Bun Monday", meaning that these were festival days with plenty of food on the table.

In most parts of Sweden, the next day has been called "Fat Tuesday", but Skåne had a couple of expressions of its own. "White Tuesday" was the name given to this day in some places, from the white – pure wheaten – flour then used for baking. Shrove Tuesday was also known in Skåne (and Småland too) as "Stonecake Tuesday", referring to the thick and hugely popular pancake originally made on heated stone slabs.

The custom of eating Shrovetide buns at this time is of course a relic of pre-Lenten gorging. The Shrovetide bun was originally a wheaten cake shaped like a thunderbolt or a wing (hence the Swedish name, *hetvägg*, which we borrowed from medieval Germany). The present-day bun, filled with cream and marzipan, is a pastry cook's concoction of the early 20th century, and the custom of eating it warm or in warm milk has a medieval pedigree.

Shrovetide, then, was for stoking up before the abstinence of Lent, and is a legacy from Catholic times. Although Denmark (which at that time included Skåne) broke with the Church of Rome already in the early 16th century, we still have many customs reminiscent of pre-Reformation times. These include certain games which are

"Beating the cat from the tun" - a popular Shrovetide game.

clearly related to the Shrovetide antics of the Mediterranean countries. In Denmark and Skåne, for example, there was tilting at the ring or "sticking the Prussian", with young men on horseback trying to capture a suspended ring with their lance or a wooden stick. This custom is doubtless modelled on the medieval tournaments. Another well-known Shrovetide game is "beating the cat from the tun". A cat would be caught and shut up in a wooden barrel which would then be suspended from the branch of a tree. The riders had to try and smash the barrel with a stick, so that the cat would fall out. The first to succeed in "liberating" the cat in this rough fashion was declared "Cat King". The custom has been revived in our own time in some parts of Skåne and Denmark, but with a doll instead of a live cat inside the barrel.

Shrovetide twigs – birch twigs on the point of budding, decorated with colourful feathers or paper rosettes – are a popular indoor decoration in Sweden at this time. In past ages people would pretend to scourge one another with the twigs before putting them in water. Two explanations have been put forward for this custom. One of them says that the twigs and the scourging are to remind us of the Passion of Our Lord, while the other says that the twigs are meant to induce fertility. But perhaps the real reason, quite simply, is that people wanted something green and decorative to embellish their homes.

Lent has been celebrated in Christian countries ever since the 5th century, to commemorate the forty days and forty nights which Jesus spent fasting in the wilderness. It begins with Ash Wednesday (the day after Shrove Tuesday), which gets its name from people metaphorically putting on sackcloth and ashes. In Catholic times this meant abstaining from eggs and meat. Fish, though, was permitted, both during Lent and in Advent.

The closing days of Lent make up *Holy Week*, which begins with *Palm Sunday*. *Maundy Thursday* in Sweden is called *Shrive Thursday*. The powers of evil were thought to be especially strong on this day, and it was now that the Easter witches were supposed to journey to the Blue Mountain. These Easter witches, it was commonly supposed, could be women versed in magic who had already sold themselves to the Devil, or

Easter letter, inscribed: "Give my hat an egg to keep, or tonight I'll never sleep."

ordinary country women who had been led astray by the Evil One. The journey was undertaken on a flying broomstick, and in southern Sweden the destination was presumed to be the island of Blå Jungfru (Blue Maiden, alias Blue Mountain) in Kalmarsund, where the Devil threw an orgy. The letting off of guns, like the bonfires lit in other parts of the country, was intended to keep the powers of evil at arm's length. Most people subscribed to these beliefs, as witness the cruel witchcraft trials that continued well into the 18th century.

Good Friday dawned grim and grave. No work was allowed unless absolutely necessary. Preferably one should also dispense with lighting the stove and make do with cold food. The women dressed themselves in black, and contrition, silence and restraint were the order of the day. This, of course, was all prompted by grief and shame over the sufferings of Christ and His death on the Cross, and in many places this atmosphere of grief on Good Friday has survived down to our own times.

One of the oddities of Swedish festivals is that we tend to celebrate them one day in advance, as for example on Christmas Eve, Easter Eve and Whit Saturday. And so we start celebrating the Resurrection already on the previous day, on Easter Saturday.

As we have already seen, Easter is the season for egg-eating, but eggs are also used as playthings. You could, for example, be voted "Egg King" in a sort of egg-conkers: if you could break your opponent's egg without breaking your own, it was yours to keep.

This custom lives on in many parts of Skåne, most famously, perhaps, in Simrishamn harbour on the morning of *Easter Day*. In many places that was also the day for egg-rolling competitions. Children would gather on a hill and carefully throw an egg (boiled) down the slope. The owner of the egg which rolled furthest without breaking took all the other eggs. This game could also be played indoors, using a corrugated tile or some other kind of chute.

We still make a habit of painting our eggs bright colours and with nice patterns before eating them at Easter. This is a centuries-old tradition and was especially widespread in Eastern Europe. Some scholars claim that painting was supposed to reinforce the power of eggs as a fertility symbol in advance of harvest time.

Easter letter with the message:
"I have tramped
with never a stop.
With greetings
from a maiden, look you.
If you don't believe me
ask the cuckoo.
When next spring you hie
To the forest nearby."

Our Lady and the first day of April

Lady Day was a holy day (holiday) until the 1953 calendar reform. It comes on 25th March, nine months before Christmas Day, and, as will be remembered, is also known as Annunciation Day, the day when Mary, despite being a virgin, became pregnant. It was the Angel Gabriel who brought the message, and by virtue of his great importance in the Bible story, he ranks as an Archangel.

Part of a painted wall-hanging, showing the Virgin Mary and the Archangel Gabriel.

In the old Julian calendar, Lady Day coincided with the Vernal Equinox, i.e. the time when day and night are of equal length. In the old agrarian society, this was an important red-letter day. Everything then had to be ready for the spring ploughing and sowing - the implements overhauled and mended, the cows let out into spring pasture and the women finished with their spinning and weaving work. In the south of Sweden, 25th March was looked on as the first real day of spring. That was the day when children were first allowed to run about barefoot, and from that day onwards people were not allowed to light candles indoors during the evening. In some places, especially in the southeast of Sweden, there was another custom associated with this day. The crane would come and put sweets in the children's stockings. This, of course, is the time of year when cranes pass over Sweden in their hundreds and thousands, making for northern Russia and Siberia.

The first of April is perhaps not all that firmly rooted as a day of practical joking in agrarian society, but it is worth dwelling on, because April foolery has a long history. April japes already existed in Sweden in the 17th century, and there are many continental parallels. A lot of these pranks are connected with the significance of "the first" or "the last", so that sometimes they were associated with the last day of March, the last day of April or the first of May.

Spring as a time of expectation, with great hopes of the future. But in many ways it was also an unpredictable, capricious time of the year, and a joke or two would help to relieve the tension. April jokes can also be said to be related to the springtime carnivals of Mediterranean countries. In both cases, All Fools' Day was a day of misrule, on which ordinary people could heckle their superiors, pulling their legs and poking fun at them, without fear of punishment. A kind of safety valve, in other words.

Walpurgis and May Day

"An old saying has it that "if Walpurgis has cold feet, there will be forty nights' more freezing." Here again, we can see how the red-letter days of the year were used as a means of looking into the future, not least weather-wise.

Walpurgis Day comes on 1st May, and not at all on the last day of April. *Walpurgis Eve* is another example of the Swedish tendency to jump the festive gun, starting one day (or at least one evening) early. Walburga (Valborg in Swedish) was an 8th century Swabian (south German – although actually she was English) Abbess and was eventually canonised for her steadfastness in the faith and her missionary zeal.

It is doubtful, though, whether the bonfires of Walpurgis Eve have really been lit, century after century, in her honour. More probably they were a ritual for scaring off the black powers of winter and darkness and predatory animals, because the next day – 1st May – was the day when cows were turned out to graze freely in the forest. Sometimes, as it Easter, the odd gunshot was fired in the direction of the forest, presumably for the same reason.

The real festival day, then, was *May Day*, with which many customs and notions are associated, both in the old agrarian society and in middle-class urban culture. In Skåne it was common to hold an "alderman meeting" on May Day, to elect the alderman or head man of the village. He led the village council which decided matters of common concern among the farmers, such as the maintenance of roads and fences, grazing on the commons and the vital matter of fire prevention in the village. The alderman meeting was also the occasion for a thundering good party which, for the quantity and quality of good cheer, was pretty well up to Christmas standard.

"May Council at the Village Stone." Watercolour by Frans Lindberg.

The village, then, would be in holiday mood around about May Day, and the youngsters took their cue, with farmers' sons and farm lads getting together to "sing in the May", going from farm to farm, singing and begging. What they were after was food (eggs were very welcome) and drink for the spring party they would be holding later. Singing as they went, they would enter the farmyard, summoning forth the inmates by banging on the door. When the master and mistress of the house appeared, the youngsters would sing, for example:

Good evening, if you're now at home!
May is now upon us.
Forgive us if too late we come:
But youth will have its honours.

More verses would follow, adding up to a wants list. If the youngsters got what they wanted, all was well and good and they would march off, warbling cheerfully, in the direction of the next farm. But if they got nothing, if the door was slammed in their face, they would yell:

Go to sleep, you mean old boor.
This is our petition:
May rooks and crows all eat you poor
And laugh you to derision.

Or words to that effect, accompanied perhaps by the lobbing of a bad egg or two at the door.

Walpurgis night and May Day have also been celebrated in the towns. For the middle class there was the Feast of the Count of May and parrot shooting, and the students of Lund and Uppsala have been arranging vocal and theatrical highjinks ever since the mid-19th century. All through the 20th century, May Day saw the labour movement on parade.

25,000 people joined the May Day marches in Malmö in 1949.

Pre-summer festivals

Forty days after Easter comes *Ascension Day*. This, then, invariably falls on a Thursday, but, like Easter, its incidence can vary by up to a month, mostly during May. It is usually a day on which people rejoice and let their hair down. In the Österlen region especially, youngsters would gather on a high point and light bonfires. From Ravlunda we are told that "on the evening before Ascension Day, it was the custom to light Ascension bonfires on the hillsides. This custom is still practised [1920s]. Right opposite Ravlunda vicarage, on the other side of the road, is a tumulus called Smedjebacken (Smith's Hill). Standing on that hill you could count anything up to 20 Ascension bonfires. Neighbouring parishes as well as Ravlunda still celebrate the festival in this way. People get together in groups and each member of the group contributes something to the bonfire."

And from Brösarp we are told: "Bonfires were lit on the hillsides on the evening before Ascension Day. More recently they were made of twigs and brushwood. When I was young [in the 1880s] we used to put up an empty tar barrel on the end of a long wooden pole. The barrel would be set alight and we would dance round it."

These fire festivals have perhaps a latter-day parallel in the early morning celebrations on Ascension Day.

Ascension Day was important for other things as well. This, for example, was when you started milking the cows three times daily. And at nightfall it was time to appoint the "good fellow" (brownie) for the year.

From Fru Alstad, we are told: "It was commonly believed that there was nothing sinful about having such a pleasant, hard working and strong little boy about the place in his red pointed hood. He always did well by his master, keeping him plentifully supplied, especially with corn. And he took good care of the livestock, going around and feeding them, especially the horses, with very small wisps of hay."

Ascension Day has also been called the first angling day. It was believed that if you stood there fishing for the whole of this day, you would learn the best time of day for fishing during the rest of the year. Another belief was that on this day you should go into the forest and count birch twigs for whisks, because the twigs are then easy to peel, and the whisks will be fine and white.

"Begging on the fox" was another custom. The following, somewhat macabre, description comes from Önnestad:

"This odd custom was still extant in Albo during the 1880s. The village youngsters would find out where there were foxes' lairs. Round about Ascension these would be dug out until fox cubs were found and caught. The youngsters would then go from one farm and cottage to another with the captured fox cubs in a basket, begging food and drink for a party. This was called a fox party. If anyone refused to pay tribute, the youngsters would threaten to let the foxes loose among the chicken."

Ten days after Ascension comes *Whitsun*, known in Swedish as the time of ecstasy, as in the case of the disciples, inspired by the Holy Ghost, speaking with tongues. In the old days this was also one of the sacrificial festivals when the parishioners had to make voluntary gifts to their church and priest.

In many parts of Skåne and elsewhere in Sweden, it was common for young women to dress up as floral or paschal brides with wreathes in their hair for the Whitsun service in a church decked with flowers. This heralded the *wreath party* with which the summer festivities began - a sequence of dance festivals every Sunday night, with all the local youngsters taking part. Often a fiddler would be engaged for these dances, and they would be held at some popular spot in the village.

"Tithe Meeting in Skåne." Painting by Bengt Nordenberg.

In other ways too, Whitsun marked the beginning of the summer, and the house was given an extra cleaning for the occasion. A lot of people would also "May" their cottages, decking them with flowers and greenery. This description, from Sjörup, refers to the early 19th century:

"Many preparations were made for celebrating Whitsun. The cottage was whitewashed, both inside and out. Cleaning meant scouring the furniture, which was white. The doors, though, were painted, and so they were washed. The windows had no curtains, curtains were something no one had ever heard of. The floor was trodden-down earth, which was dusted and strewn with juniper twigs chopped fine. Fresh beech leaves were fastened to the loft inside the cottage when all the other decorations were ready.

"Cakes were baked. For a real feast there were sponge cakes, stone cakes, waffles and egg cakes. These last had to be eaten on Whit Saturday, and the others were for visitors. Another very common thing was that there had to be chicken soup for dinner on Whit Sunday."

The Scanian funnel cake

Professor Emeritus Nils-Arvid Bringéus rates the funnel cake *(spettkaka)*, together with the goose and the eel, as the foremost among Scanian delicacies. It is hard to disagree.

On the other hand, the funnel cake is not a Scanian speciality by origin. Some have traced it back to 16th century Germany, others all the way to classical antiquity. To make matters worse, it came to its rightful home by way of Stockholm.

Skåne has all the prerequisites of a good funnel cake culture – an abundance of eggs, potatoes, sugar, big farmers and big parties – and the funnel cake has evolved here into a symbol of Scanian prosperity. At first funnel cakes were made in manor houses and vicarages, but eventually the technique and the custom filtered down to ordinary farm houses. At the beginning of the 19th century the funnel cake was quite a common ingredient of wedding festivities in Skåne. At really big parties there could be anything up to a dozen of them on show.

It is hard to say, of course, where the first Scanian funnel cake was baked, but several sources point in favour of the wife of a Dutch head gardener at Torup.

The funnel cake can be described as a tall, cone-shaped, meringue-like composition, encrusted with icing and made from a batter of eggs, sugar and potato flour. But of course, it is far more than that. The pristine version is personally crafted, revealing to the expert not only where the cake comes from but even who made it.

A real funnel cake, of course, has to be circled – "meddled" – by hand at the open fire. The baker builds up his funnel cake by winding it and drizzling on the batter with a careful, steady hand. When the mixture has dried, the cake is slowly turned over the fire to give it an even colour. Towards the end of the process you have to turn faster, so that the batter stays on the surface, forming strips. These strips are the signature of the master: the longer they are, the more excellent the cake. Slowly but surely the delicacy evolves. Much of its beauty lies in the irregularity of the pattern. The icing comes last, and in the old days this is what told you where in Skåne the cake had been made. In Genarp, for example, their funnel cakes were all white, while in the Österlen region a funnel cake

could be tricked out with white, pink and green icing.

Although the technique of making a *spettkaka* was common knowledge, by no means all farms used to make their own.

There were always "funnel cake grannies" in the neighbourhood who would make one in return for payment, often using the customer's own eggs.

A 100-piece funnel cake takes two score eggs to make and is more than enough for a flash party. Lund Spettkaksbageri issues the following instructions for the gutting of the delicacy: "When cutting, start from the bottom and make a horizontal cut right through the cake. Divide this lower part into suitable pieces as preferred. The upper part then remains intact, like a decorative but reduced *spettkaka* for the next 'pruning'... The tailings of the cake, served with whipped cream, make a very good dessert. Quite simply, you make a meringue Suisse, but using funnel cake instead of meringues." Another technique is to cut out windows by plunging the pointed saw into the body of the cake, making two vertical incisions and then with two quick horizontal ones to detach a whole piece.

Spettkaka goes very well with ice cream or sharp-tasting fruit. Nowadays it is often served with coffee, but try it with a glass of sherry.

Most funnel cakes today are more or less factory made, several cakes at a time on a single shaft over an electric heat source. But seekers will find that there are still "funnel cake grannies" well-versed in the traditional method. You could take your own eggs.

"The wedding feast." Watercolour by Frans Lindberg.

Funnel cakes on parade at the 1914 Baltic Exhibition, which among other things featured works of decorative art from Sweden, Denmark, Germany and Russia. The tasties in this picture come from parts of Skåne and show the characteristic features associated with their places of origin. The best thing of all about the spettkaka is that it makes a feast for the palate as well as the eye. Some things never change.

HERRING PANCAKES

on a sautéed salad of early spring vegetables

Serves 4

INGREDIENTS:

5 dl milk
25 g yeast (1/2 packet)
2 dl coarse flour, e.g. rye flour
1 egg
2-3 salted herring fillets, soaked and drained
salt, pepper
sugar to taste
cooking fat for frying
Accessories: early spring vegetables, e.g. young carrots, mange-tout, Welsh onion.

PROCEDURE:

1. Warm the milk to blood heat and dissolve the yeast in it.
2. Stir in the flour and run the mixture until quite smooth, using a stick blender if you have one.
3. Fold in the egg and leave the mixture to rise for about 30 minutes.
4. Meanwhile, chop the herring fine, then fold it in the dough and give it another burst with the blender.
5. Add salt and pepper to taste and, for contrast, just a pinch of sugar.
6. Fry in a cast iron griddle, using just a little fat.
7. Peel and cut up the different vegetables
8. Serve with the spring vegetables and a daub of crème fraîche.

COOK'S COMMENT

By the time spring arrived, larders were usually pretty empty. Perhaps there were just a few fragments of salt herring left over. Using up leftovers was essential for keeping body and soul together all the year round. Because hens came into lay at springtime, I think this pancake composition is a fine example of traditional home cooking in springtime.

TERRINE OF COARSE FISH LIKE ROACH AND IDE

Served with a nettle dressing

Serves 4

INGREDIENTS:

450–500 g fillets of "scrap fish" like roach, ide etc.
1/2 onion
2 eggs
a bunch of thyme
1 dl milk
salt and pepper
grease for the mould
10–12 slices of gravlax
1 head of fresh spinach
1 handful of small nettles (not more than 2 cm high)
2 tbs. cooking oil
1/2 tbs. vinegar (of some exciting kind)

PROCEDURE:

For this dish you need a meat grinder or food processor and an oblong, oven-proof mould or loaf tin.

1. Skin and fillet the fish as best you can, removing all large bones if possible.
2. Peel and divide the onion.
3. Using the finest disk in the grinder, put the fish and onion through at least twice, to be sure of crushing any bones that are still there.
4. Mix with the eggs and thyme. Dilute with milk and then add salt and pepper to taste. (Of course you can spit out afterwards!)
5. Grease a 1.5 litre loaf tin and place the salmon slices in it so that they cover the bottom and hang over the sides a little. Fill half way up with the fish mixture and 5–6 well-rinsed spinach leaves, topped up with the rest of the fish and fold over the gravlax slices to make a package.
6. Bake in the oven at 100°C for about an hour or until you sense a certain firmness in the terrine. You can also measure the inside temperature with an oven thermometer. At 90°C the terrine is ready.
7. Leave the terrine to cool in the loaf tin for an hour or so in the fridge, so that it will settle down to a more homogeneous, firm consistency. Then, after working gently round the edges with a knife, tip out carefully.
8. Run the nettles in a food processor together with the oil and vinegar. Add just a little salt and pepper to taste.
9. Serve the terrine on an attractive bed of lettuce with the dressing, and all of a sudden you have turned the uneatable into a gastronomic experience.

SALMON OMELETTE WITH MUSTARD AND CHIVES

served with raw-fried, roasted root vegetables

Serves 4 at breakfast

INGREDIENTS:
1/2 carrot
1/2 parsnip
1/2 celeriac
1 small bunch of chives
6 eggs
1/2 dl milk
1 tsp. Skåne mustard
salt and pepper
fat for frying
about 200 g raw, smoked, lightly salted or gravlax salmon fillet, cut in small pieces

PROCEDURE:
1. Peel and dice the root vegetables. Chop the chives very small.
2. Roast the root vegetables by frying them without fat, on a fairly high flame, in a frying pan until they have softened and turned a nice colour.
3. Beat the omelette mixture – eggs and milk – together, fold in the mustard and chives and add salt and pepper to taste. (Go easy on the salt if you are using salted salmon or gravlax.)
4. Melt a little fat in an omelette pan to fry the pieces of salmon. Pour on the omelette mixture and keep stirring until it begins to set.
5. When nearly all the mixture has set, scrape the whole omelette onto the half of the pan which is furthest from the handle. Try to build it up as high as possible. Leave it there for a minute or two, to solidify properly. Transfer to a plate by holding the plate over the omelette and then turning the whole thing upside down.
6. Serve the salmon omelette with the roasted root vegetables.

COOK'S COMMENT

Salted food was eaten for most of the year, and so eggs made a very welcome change. An omelette flavoured with gravlax will do excellently for a hearty breakfast, lunch or a light dinner.

SALMON SUNFLOWER

with salmon roe and egg yolk

Serves 4

INGREDIENTS:
500 g fresh filleted salmon
100 g salmon roe
4 egg yolks
one or two twists of the pepper mill
one pinch of salt

PROCEDURE:
1. Slice the salmon as thin as possible. (Just like gravlax or smoked salmon.)
2. Lay the slices flat on a plate but leave room in the middle for the egg yolk with the salmon roe enclosing it.
3. Scatter a little salt, give two turns of the pepper mill over the salmon, and your starter is ready.

COOK'S COMMENT

To eliminate hostile bacteria, all raw products should be frozen before use. If you do this there is no danger in eating raw fish. And you don't have to be Japanese to enjoy it!

MINT-MARINATED FILLET OF LAMB

on a salad of sheep's milk cheese and lamb herbs

Serves 4

INGREDIENTS:

500 g fillet of lamb
1 bunch of mint
1/2 dl cooking oil (preferably cold-pressed rape-seed oil from Österlen)
1 dl salt
3 dl sugar
4–5 turns of white pepper from the pepper mill
5 tbsp. brandy
5 tbsp. madeira
1 bunch of basil
1 bunch of thyme
1 bunch of sage
salt, sugar
200 g. sheep's cheese, sliced

PROCEDURE:

Marinate the lamb two or three days in advance.

1. Remove all sinews from the meat.
2. Tear half the mint leaves and run them in a food processor with one or two tsp. oil.
3. Put the meat in double plastic bags. Pour in salt, sugar, brandy, madeira and the mint oil. Tie up and leave on a plate in the fridge for about 2 or 3 days, turning occasionally.
4. On the serving day, mix all the herbs into a salad. Pour on oil, salt and sugar. Slice the marinated lamb and serve with the herb salad and a little sliced sheep's milk cheese. (If you prefer, or if necessary, eke out the herb salad with various kinds of ordinary lettuce.)

GRILLED LAMB

with a red and yellow tomato salad gratinated with basil and served with a purée of celeriac

Serves 4

INGREDIENTS:
1 celeriac
1 tbsp. butter
salt, pepper
3 red tomatoes
3 yellow tomatoes
2 dl cooking oil
1 pot/bunch of basil
600 g lamb chops, entrecôte or fillet, sliced

PROCEDURE:
A stick blender is ideal for this recipe.
1. Set the oven to 200°C.
2. Peel the celeriac and cut in small pieces. Boil it in lightly salted water in a saucepan until it is really soft.
3. Drain the celeriac and mash it with a stick blender or by some other means. Add a knob of butter and salt and pepper to taste.
4. Slice the tomatoes and put them on an oven-proof dish in four piles, with yellow and red mixed.
5. Mix the oil and basil, adding a little salt and pepper. Pour this over the tomatoes and bake in the upper half of the oven till the tomatoes have turned a nice colour.
6. Meanwhile grill the lamb under the grill or in a grill pan, or else just fry it in an ordinary frying pan on a high flame for a short time. Salt and pepper.
7. Package the meat in grease-proof/baking tray paper and leave it to rest.
8. Serve the meat on plates with the luke warm tomato and basil salad and the purée of celeriac.

SUMMER

A longed-for coolness...

A longed-for coolness towards evening
for the house and the animals
the sheep in the shade of the beeches
rose to their feet: small steamers
puffing out air
now move grazing
deep in the clover
knowing the night
is nothing to fear.

The hills promise more light
grass and children
I lie on my back
in the shade of the house
and so the days lumber along
when summer gathered at last.

CARL MAGNUS VON SETH
From "Land du välsignade", 1993

Summer food

May brings in the summer season, tentatively at first but getting more sure of itself as time goes on. This opens the door to a whole new larder, consisting initially of eggs and milk but also including products from your own garden and everyone's forest.

Where firstlings and gardening are concerned, Skåne is one step ahead of regions further north. The climate is more hospitable, which makes for a wider and earlier selection of crops. Historically, Skåne has been the first recipient of new developments from further south. Monasticism and feudalism touched down here before advancing further into Scandinavia. The same goes for the Scanian concept of the vegetable and herb garden.

This kitchen garden gave both nurture and ornament – flowerbeds rubbing shoulders, as it were, with herbs and vegetables. Where roots and green vegetables are concerned, cabbage has been the mainstay of the Scanian diet. Already in medieval times, both town and country had plots of white and green (spring) cabbage for soups and broths and for the hugely popular *långkål* (Skåne kale), which was mostly eaten in winter and above all at Christmas. (To make *långkål*, boil green cabbage in ham stock till it softens. Then chop it, heat in a frying pan with butter and flavour with salt, sugar, treacle and white pepper.) Carrots too were often used in soups, but for other things as well. Bothilda Nilsson of Bontofta, reminiscing in 1928, recalls, "The butter was coloured with carrots. They were grated and juice poured into the cream to turn the butter a nice shade of yellow." For the same reason, both carrots and beetroot were sliced and tipped into the brewing vat, turning the small beer a mellow dark brown.

In Skåne, it was propitious for particular crops to be sown on particular days. In Fru Alstad, for example, onions, mustard, lettuce, parsley, thyme, marjoram, leeks, cabbage and kohlrabi had to be sown before Walpurgis. Carrots and beetroot, on the other hand, had to be sown just before 27th May ("Beda Day"), while beans, cucumbers and marrows had to be planted on the day itself.

The rule about sowing beans on Annunciation Day is mentioned in any number of records, and the rule about sowing peas on St Erik's day (18th May), seems almost as common. Peas, incidentally, were not only for eating an informant in Hofterup points out: "Anyone with toothache must keep some peas in his mouth when the tooth hurts most. Then he must try to throw the peas in the neighbour's well without anyone seeing. If he succeeds, his toothache will disappear." Passed on to the hapless neighbour presumably. Another ancient rule says that beans and peas have to be boiled in "running" water, meaning water taken from a watercourse of some kind. That way they turned out best.

Other garden plants were also for the soups which were so commonly served. In summer, the new beetroot, carrots, parsnips and turnips would be sliced and put into the soup together with a fragment of meat, a cut of the salt pork or a pair of green-salted herring. Probably all these root vegetables were introduced by the monks in medieval times. After the

Reformation, when the monasteries were dissolved, they were mainly grown in castle gardens, becoming staple produce in the 18th and 19th centuries. The big estates, as well as vicarages, played an important part in disseminating new developments, not least as regards produce, cooking and culinary fashion.

The potato became an increasingly vital component of ordinary people's diet in the 19th century. Especially popular, according to a note from Stoby, was "ashed potatoes".

Left-over boiled potatoes, whole and unpeeled were laid in the hot ashes on the kitchen stove if there was one, or in the baking oven if it happened to be still warm. Potatoes done this way were eaten unpeeled. With them you had roast herring. Salt herring was put to soak for an hour or so and then put straight on the embers in the fireplace and turned over with the fire tongs.

But don't suppose for one minute that potatoes superseded the venerable turnip. Ever since medieval times, turnips, especially the delicate Maytime variety, had been an ingredient for soups, whereas the potato became a separate adjunct to boiled, fried or roast meat (or fish) on the plate. In addition, potatoes came to be used more and more for distilling.

But vegetables were not all that came out of the kitchen garden. There were currants (red ones mostly), gooseberries, raspberries and, eventually, strawberries. The currants were mostly turned into squash and jam, while the gooseberries were often stewed or made into marmalade. Gooseberry bushes had a secondary use. "To make the child's hair curl, after the christening, which usually took place at home, you had to empty the christening bowl over a gooseberry bush." This description comes from Örkened.

The red colour of raspberry could inspire notions of sympathetic magic.

"Johanna, my eldest girl, was born with a raspberry just over her right eye. When I was expecting her I had gone picking raspberries and one got into my right eye. To get rid of it the mother has to first blow to the right and left of the mark and then straight at it, and then open her mouth over it on 40 mornings on an empty stomach." This M.O. comes from Frosta.

Gardens had also included at least one or two elderberry bushes. Both flowers and berries would be turned into squash and jam, but the elderberry bush is also the focus of a good many popular beliefs. A mystical female being, Hyllemor, lived underneath the bush, and she was somebody you had to keep well in with. If, for example, you happened to let water on an elderberry bush, you were in big trouble. Hyllemor would immediately pay you back with toothache, itching or some other complaint. In Harlösa the belief was that if an expectant mother "polluted an elderberry bush, the child would come out in a rash" and that falling asleep there was sure to give you headache. If someone had been lying down under an elderberry bush and

got a headache, people in Skurup would say that "Hyllemor had drugged him." Elderflowers could also be boiled in unstrained milk and drunk as a cure for toothache.

In or adjoining the garden there were fruit trees, mostly apple, pear and plum.

Somebody in Stoby recalls: "You didn't buy fruit trees, instead you fetched wild apple from the forest and grafted it. Wild apple trees were brought into the garden in the autumn, or else planted along fences or roadsides near the buildings. After they had taken root and grown to the right size, they were grafted. The commonest type of apple were Kalmar Glass, red and white Astrakhan, White Gyllen, Rosenhäger, Gravenstein and Järnäpple (good eating at Eastertime).

The main pear varieties grown were August pears, *pellemott* (Bergamotte), "Swan Neck" and "Grey Pears" (*gråpäron*). In the north of Skåne, pears were humorously termed "tree pears" as distinct from "earth pears" (potatoes).

The fruit was, of course, used fresh for desserts of different kinds, but it could also be preserved in a variety of ways. Apples and pears were mostly dried.

A lady from Västra Göinge recalls: "My mother used to pack the apples in fine-chopped straw in a big chest. That way they would keep until March or April. Apples and pears were also dried in quite large quantities. The fruit was peeled, cut up, decored, put on baking trays and dried in the baking oven, which would be just the right temperature after bread-making. This dried fruit was kept in linen bags which were hung from the roof beams in the attic."

An ancient rule said that when picking fruit you must never strip the tree completely: you must always leave one or two apples, pears or plums on it. We don't know exactly why this had to be so. Perhaps it was a kind of "rainy day" principle. Or perhaps it was a magical way of promoting next year's growth by sacrificing the last of this year's.

Onion, mustard and herbs also had their appointed places in the kitchen garden. Onion was used for cooking, but not only that. In Sankt Olof, for example: "People ate onion, both raw, boiled and fried, because onions were medicine and purified the blood, so the old folk said." Mustard is a distinctively Scanian herb: nowhere else in Sweden is it grown and eaten in such quantities. Both pork and fish were often served with mustard sauce, and people in Skåne still insist on mustard sauce with their Yuletide *lutfisk* (made from dried ling).

Another distinctive feature of traditional Scanian food is strong flavouring, – spiced herring, for example. Thyme was grown in the gardens for pea soup, but also, as it was recorded in Stoby, because "thyme gave you pure blood, free from toxic substances, and a lot of girls drank tea made from thyme and were made pretty by it (if they were pretty before), and it was believed that by drinking tea made from thyme they could stay young."

Marjoram, hyssop, caraway (for bread and cheese, but also for *brännesnuda*) lavender, coriander, spearmint, sage and of course wormwood were also to be found in the gardens of most farmhouses. Wormwood, in linen bags, was put in between the clothes in a clothes chest, but, if we are to believe an informant from Skurup, it was above all used for flavouring schnapps:

"From the bunches of wormwood you picked out small twigs and made 'wormwood bitters' by simply pushing the twigs into a bottle past the cork, leaving it to stand and then topping up when it became too strong, though you could also strip off the buds in schnapps which you set light to, strained and then mixed with a suitable quantity of ordinary schnapps."

These spices were used in other ways too, as somebody from Allerum tells us. "People were afraid of letting out heat in winter, so to improve the air they would take a few sage and rose leaves that had been salted down in a big earthenware jar and put them on the oven to make a nice smell. I think they sometimes included lavender as well."

Various goodies were harvested from the forest and roadside as well during summer. In northern Skåne especially, lingonberries and blueberries were picked in large quantities. Nils Jönsson, born in Önnestad in 1878, takes up the story:

"Picking lingonberries on a fine day in late summer was very enjoyable. I would go into the forest with the servant girls and children from the farm. We would take with us plenty to eat. The berries we picked went into small chip baskets, and they were emptied into the lovely flat-bottomed straw baskets that nowadays you only see in local heritage museums. Often the harvest was so big that a horse and cart had to be fetched to carry it home. Lingonberry property rights were respected a lot more then than they are today. Berry thieves were pretty uncommon."

During the summer season, daylight and with it the working day, lasted longer than in winter, and so there were more meals in summertime to keep people's strength up. From Åkarp we have the following mealtime programme for the hay-making season:

"4 o'clock Coffee and bread.
8 o'clock Breakfast with stewed herring pancakes, small beer.
12 o'clock Dinner, consisting of boiled food.
4 o'clock Evening meal consisting of bread and butter and milk and water.
9 o'clock Supper, consisting of porridge and milk.
There was rum toddy to drink when the hay-making was finished."

A more detailed description has come down to us from Göinge:

"Breakfast usually consisted of fried potatoes, warmed up 'potato porridge' or rye meal porridge left over from the previous day, fried pork or *spickesill*, butter or dripping and bread and skimmed milk or small beer. Dinner: nothing but pea soup and pancakes on Thursday, otherwise a kind of meat soup, potato purée, bread soup (meaning cubes of bread in small beer which had been brought to the boil with treacle added and thickened with milk and potato flour) or lingonberry (cowberry) jam with milk. Occasionally there would be rice pudding. For the evening meal there would be coffee with sandwiches and cheese. Supper was boiled potatoes with herring and some kind of 'dip', rye meal porridge with butter or treacle in the middle, bread, butter or dripping and milk. On Sundays there would often be fricassée with peeled potatoes, brown beans or string beans with fried pork, rice pudding or fruit soup of some kind. These were the commonest dishes."

Midsummer

As a result of the 1953 calendar reform, Midsummer's Eve always falls on the Friday nearest 23rd June. Previously Midsummer's Eve was celebrated on that very date, and it still is in Denmark and Norway, where the festival is known as St Hans' Eve (after John - Johannes – the Baptist).

The foremost symbol of midsummer, the maypole, is known in Scandinavia from the 15th century. It is probably of German origin, and it was long the custom for the maypoles to be left standing all the year round in towns and big villages. Perhaps the custom of raising a maypole (decorated with leaves and flowers) had some connection with a fertility rite, the idea being for the pole and the dancing round it to bring a good harvest. Consequently a lot of clergy protested against this heathen custom during the 18th and 19th centuries. Nowadays, dancing round the maypole to songs like "Small Frogs" and "Cutting Oats" is mainly for the children, while young adults, as is well known, tend to reserve their energies for another dance floor later on, in the evening.

In Skåne and Blekinge, as well as in Bohuslän, Jämtland and Härjedalen, the former Danish and

Maypole at Rydsgård, 1929.

Norwegian provinces respectively, it was customary to light a midsummer fire, the St Hans bonfire.

Midsummer Eve was one of the most important festivals of the year, an occasion when one could look into the future and perhaps try to do something about it. A record from Eslöv has it that if you could stay awake all Midsummer's Eve, you wouldn't be drowsy for the rest of the year.

There was any amount of good advice and rules about harnessing the power of Midsummer's Eve to cure or avert different illnesses. If you broke off a twig of mugwort and tucked it inside your shirt, this would fend off cancer, and if you cut nine whistles of elderberry twigs and blew them over rashes and eczema, these would disappear. The dew of Midsummer Night was considered especially potent. To obtain an effective medicine for most ailments, you had to spread out a linen cloth in the churchyard during the evening. Then on the morning of Midsummer's Day you would wring out the dew into a bottle and you were recommended to spice this with schnapps. A still more effective cure could be achieved by completely wrapping the patient in the cloth and leaving it to dry on his bare body.

Then there was the well-known prophecy of one's husband-to-be. From Norra Nöbbelöv we are told:

"The girls used to pick nine different flowers after sunset and put them under their pillows. Whoever they then dreamed of would be their husband. There was another way too in which girls could see their future husband. After they had undressed they were to eat a whole herring - ungutted and undried - without telling anyone. Whoever came to them that night with water was their husband-to-be." The nine flowers – seven, according to some sources – also had another use, according to an informant in Äsphult: "For fumigating people and livestock that were ill, you had to collect nine different herbs on Midsummer's Night and dry them. They were then burned on a small fire, over which the patient had to sit, so that the smoke would reach the evil."

You could also put the flowers underneath the stones by the entrance to the shippon, to protect the livestock from witchcraft.

Midsummer provided a welcome break from work and there are innumerable written records of how it was celebrated. The following comes from Löderup in about 1880:

"Farmhands made a maypole out of a 12-ell pole and fitted it with two cross-pieces about three ells from the top. The younger lads cut leafy twigs in the park. Boys and girls walked out to the Fröslöv hills and fields to pick sticky catchfly, lady's bedstraw, cornflower, oxeye daisies and buttercups. They all helped to make garlands of flowers and leaves and decorate the maypole overall with twigs and wild flowers. At the top of the pole they fastened a strip of cloth to serve as a flag. The pole was then lowered to a hole in the ground in the middle of the farmyard. First, though, the hole was lined with stones then the pole was braced with four props.

"Between 4 and 6 o'clock on Midsummer's Eve, youngsters from round about came to Gyllerup for dancing. The lads wore boots and leather trousers, sleeveless waistcoats and peaked caps. The girls had on shoes or slippers of leather, blue or black stockings and full broadcloth skirts with bodices. They wore silk scarves on their heads.

"The leading farmhand would engage a fiddler to play for the party. The commonest dances were the waltz, the swing dance, the polska and the quadrille."

Even nowadays, the Midsummer holiday is the undisputed climax of the summer season, and in Sweden it has achieved a very set form, with maypole and dancing, herring, schnapps and new potatoes, a festival with no counterpart outside Sweden and the Swedish-speaking part of Finland. As a result, Midsummer in many people's eyes has become quintessentially Swedish.

From small-scale production to central distilleries

In the 18th century, schnapps was commonly believed to be highly nourishing, made as it was from cereals. Linnaeus, among others, did his best to scotch the idea.

Schnapps was also believed to be good for you for other reasons. It was a cure for various ills. As such it had to be strong, fiery and bitter, and if it had a nasty taste, so much the better. The description was equally suited to schnapps, beaver droppings, camphor, salt, tar and garlic. You paid your money and you took your choice.

Wormwood schnapps was the commonest variety, especially for stomach complaints. Black currant schnapps and camphor schnapps were good for colds, not to mention all the other variants.

Schnapps at the beginning of the 19th century was part of the everyday household economy. The farmer would usually start the day with a glass of bitters, often before he had even got out of bed. Second breakfast and the evening meal were washed down with schnapps, and a dram would also be taken with the two principal meals of the day – dinner and supper.

Home distilling was finally abolished between 1855 and 1860. This, coupled with the appearance of coffee, helped to create an entirely new pattern of consumption. But schnapps did not vanish from the scene completely. Very often the morning dram was replaced with "strong" coffee.

Vin- & ~ Spirituosa

handeln

Tyringe,

adr. **Tyringe,**
försäljer
absolut 10-dubb. renadt bränvin vid köp af minst 50 liter fraktfritt vid alla järnvägsstationer i Sverige för 80 öre pr liter.
50 liter ovanligt god Cognac erhålles med fritt ekkärl fraktfritt för 50 kr

At the same time as home distilling was prohibited, the distilleries came under government control. National distilleries had existed earlier, as far back as the 15th century, but for the production of gunpowder.

It was not the prohibition itself that led to an upsurge of factory distilling. The distilleries had been developing all through the 19th century. Quite a number of technical innovations, for example, came to Skåne from Germany. One of the pioneers at this time was the physicist Benjamin Thompson (Count Rumford), who among other things discovered that a liquid could be made to boil by infusing it with steam. This made it possible to reduce the number of distillations from two to one. Another important invention was the mash heater, which helped reduce consumption of firewood during the process. Then, when Frans Ernst Siemens developed a pressure cooker, the foundations of industrialised distilling were laid.

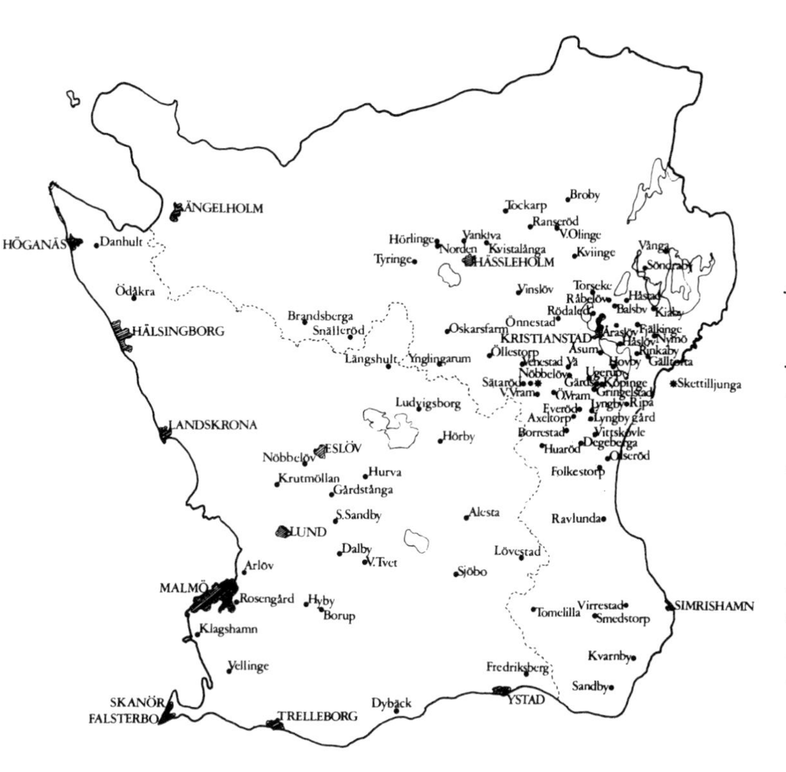

No fewer than 86 distilleries in Skåne joined Swedish Distillers' Association at its formation in 1907. Altogether the Association represented 118 different distilleries in Sweden, accounting between them for about 90 per cent of national schnapps production. From "Skånskt Brännvin".

The County of Kristianstad already acquired four steam distilleries in 1837, at Hagestadsborg, Vegeholm, Marielund and Glimminge. At the same time the Svenstorp steam distillery opened outside Lund. By 1852 the Counties of Kristianstad and Malmöhus between them had 199 steam distilleries, and a little over 20 years later these two counties were providing more than 40 per cent of Sweden's entire output of schnapps.

In 1907 there were 86 Scanian distilleries affiliated to the newly formed Swedish Distillers' Association. The Association's total membership of 118 accounted for 90 per cent of all schnapps production in Sweden. The Association did well by the Scanian distilling industry, partly by keeping prices up.

At the outbreak of the First World War Skåne had 100 distilleries. During the 1920s, potato schnapps was ousted by sulphite spirit. The government began to consider a concentration of manufacturing facilities, and a big step in that direction came with the report of the 1946 Spirits Commission. Another came with the report of the Potato Commission in 1953. The last campaign, in 1970/71, found 32 distilleries remaining in Skåne. A year later there were just two, with a total output of 27 million crude spirit - one in Tomelilla and the other, the Gärdsnäs Distillery, outside Kristianstad.

THE OWNER,
of certain items of spirits left here on Christmas Eve can recover the same for the price of this advertisement.
Höganäs 4th March

N. P. Andersson's Cigar Shop
Upper Höganäs

Food and music in the countryside

Songs directly referring to food are more in student vein and were never heard during mealtimes at Scanian hostelries. On the other hand a lot of instrumental music was played during meals. The fiddlers would reel off the whole of their repertoire, sometimes two or three times over, before sending round the plate.

After an intermission it was time for dancing, and the fiddlers were back on duty again. Most dances took place in the yard, not infrequently with a great deal of leaping and kicking. All that food had to be shaken down somehow! Most often the music was provided by just one or two fiddlers, and the repertoire was always the same, no matter who played. New tunes gradually insinuated themselves, but this was a slow process. The commonest instruments were the violin, clarinet and flute. The accordion came on the scene a few years into the 19th century.

In the 18th and 19th centuries there were fiddlers of the hundred and parish who were privileged and authorised to provide the music and be paid for it. Unauthorised music could mean a court case and damages. The fiddlers formed a guild of their own, issuing their own charters.

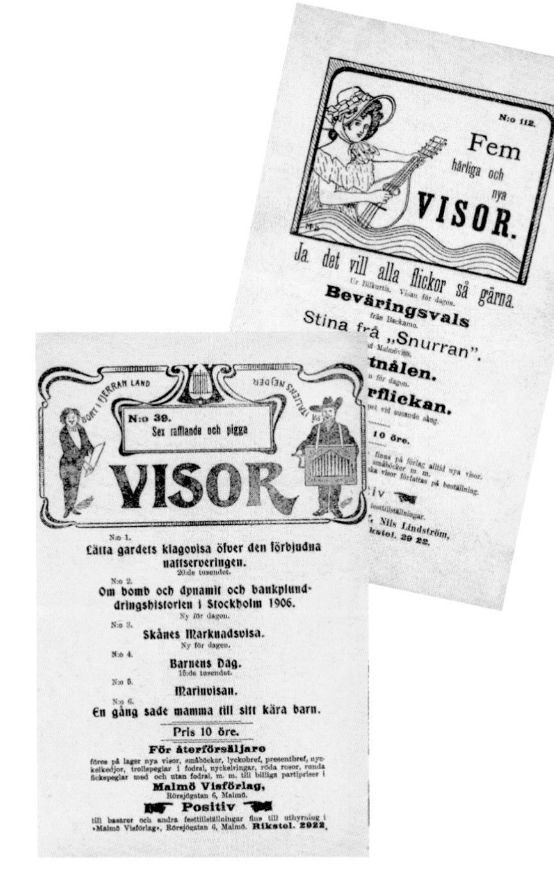

N:o 112.
Fem härliga och nya VISOR.
Ja det vill alla flickor så gärna.
Ur Bilkurtis. Visan för dagen.
Beväringsvals
från Backamo.
Stina frå „Snurran".

N:o 39.
Sex rafflande och pigga
VISOR

Bort i fjerran land
Italiens mejder

N:o 1.
Lätta gardets klagovisa öfver den förbjudna nattserveringen.
20:de tusendet.
N:o 2.
Om bomb och dynamit och bankplundringshistorien i Stockholm 1906.
Ny för dagen.
N:o 3.
Skånes Marknadsvisa.
Ny för dagen.
N:o 4.
Barnens Dag.
15:de tusendet.
N:o 5.
Marinvisan.
N:o 6.
En gång sade mamma till sitt kära barn.

Pris 10 öre.

För återförsäljare
föres på lager nya visor, småböckar, lyckobref, presentbref, nyckelkedjor, trollspeglar i fodral, nyckelringar, röda rosor, runda fickspeglar med och utan fodral, m. m. till billiga partipriser i
Malmö Visförlag,
Rörsjögatan 6, Malmö.
Positiv
till basarer och andra festtillställningar fins till uthyrning i »Malmö Visförlag», Rörsjögatan 6, Malmö. Rikstel. 2922.

The shortest distance between two human beings is dance music on a summer's evening. It always has been and so it always will be. If there was no orchestra, you sang yourself. To help you there were any number of song books. Here is one published in Malmö in 1905, and another from 1915.

"Dance Floor among the Bushes" 1920s.

Harvest home at Rösjöholm, 1908. The lads on the right and the girls on the left.

Guilds meant journeymen, and so the succession was well provided for.

Music of a general character was not all that was played at parties. Rounds were struck up when there were toasts to be drunk. People "figured" at each other, in time to the music. "It sounded like fanfares coming from the violins," we are told.

Pretexts for parties were never lacking, whether on the farm or at the classier hostelry. Some of the recurrent, most written-about parties and festivals were:

The Straw Party, at the end of the spring ploughing.
The Muck Party, at the end of May, after the fallow fields had been manured.
The May Singing Party.
The Cat Party at Whitsun, when the cat was knocked out of the barrel.
The Topping Out Party, after the timbers had been raised for a new house.
The Wash Party, for a big laundry session at the waterside.
The Carding Party, when it was time to scutch the flax.
The Snigging Party, after hauling timber from the forest.
The Hay Rack Party, after the hay racks had been put up in the fields.
The Harvest Home.
The Christmas Feast.
The Autumn Feast took place when all the harvest had been put away in the barns.
The Bondagers' Party was a marathon bash for the farm workers of both sexes, lasting anything from three to six days.

The Crayfish party at the end of summer

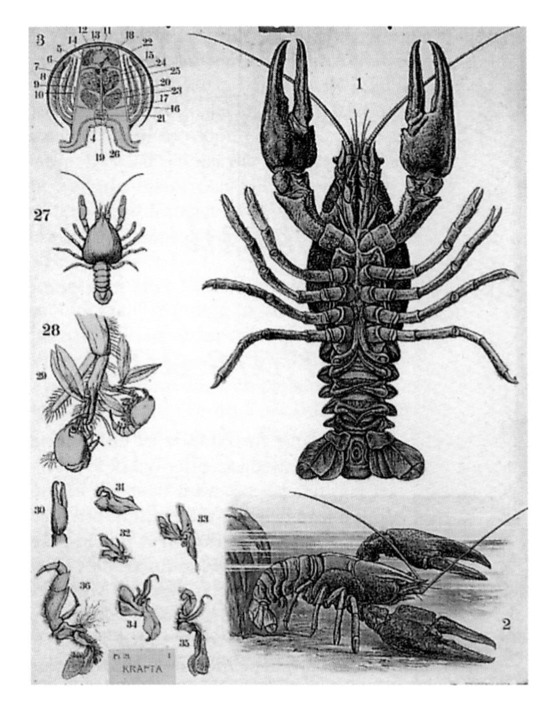

What can be more typically Swedish than a crayfish party in a lilac arbour? The natural scenery, the schnapps and the ditties extend the limits of the permissible. The participants know what to expect in the way of menu and accessories, and the rite is supervised only by the moon, be it a cardboard image or the real article. The crayfish party has become almost a manifestation of Swedishness, on a par with Midsummer, Christmas and Lucia. But crayfish-eating in Sweden doesn't really go back all that far. Up until just over a hundred years ago, crayfish were only appreciated by the upper crust, and then in the form of concoctions like crayfish in aspic, fricassée of crayfish and even crayfish tart.

The Swedish farmers didn't eat crayfish. If anything they were rather averse to them. Crayfish were mysterious carrion-eaters, and they crawled backwards. Round about the turn of the century, crayfish attracted the attention of a rapidly expanding middle class. Crayfish suppers were thrown on verandas and in arbours at summer retreats. Outdoor eating quickly resulted in the crayfish being served cold and with the late summer season's own firstling, heads of dill. It was now that the party began to be illuminated with lanterns and moons, and so the modern crayfish party was born.

But the crayfish party did not become a really universal Swedish custom until after the Second World War. By then leisure had become law, and greater prosperity caused many upper-class habits to spread further down the social scale. Crayfish became an August imperative. But here, as in so many other such instances, the farmers were the last to catch on.

The crayfish party isn't just typically Swedish, it's uniquely Swedish. True, crayfish are caught and eaten in other countries as well, but there they are neither caught, cooked nor eaten in the same way as in Sweden. The Swedish concept of the crayfish party has no real equivalent anywhere else.

Crayfish have to be eaten as summer changes into autumn. Everyone agrees on that, even though refrigeration technology has long since made it possible for them to be eaten at any time of the year, and even though firms in the 1990s did their best to market "high summer crayfish" already at Midsummer. The crayfish party is not just an ordinary shellfish supper, which perhaps explains why it has grown so popular. It has become something of a "kids' party for grown-ups", an occasion when you are allowed to be childish and make a fool of yourself, get a little bit tipsy and sing rude songs, eat with your fingers, slurp and flout most of the traditional rules of etiquette.

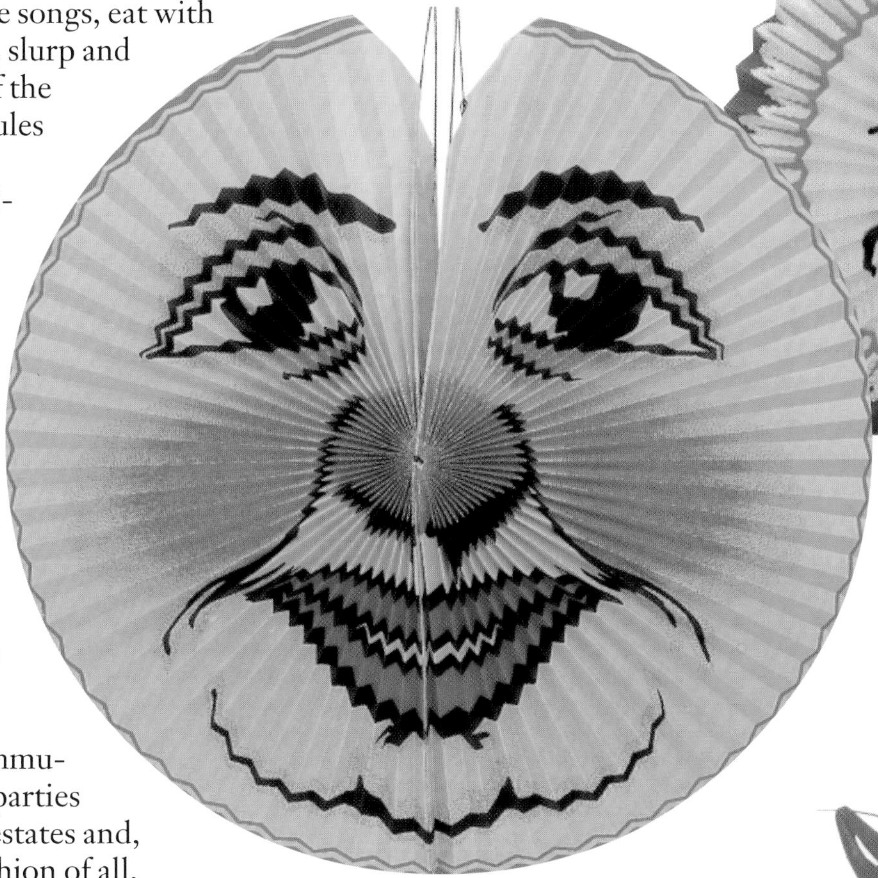

The carnival atmosphere has also resulted in the crayfish party assuming more public manifestations in recent years, such as staff parties with crayfish, communal crayfish parties on housing estates and, the latest fashion of all, mammoth parties at which people buy a few crayfish and a can of beer, bring their own schnapps and sit down at immensely long tables often together with complete strangers in whose company one is expected to experience both enjoyment and cohesion. The crayfish party during the Malmö Festival ("traditional" since 1986) is probably the biggest of them all, with the participants getting through nearly 100,000 crayfish in one sitting.

Obviously, the crayfish party in this carnival form has come to resemble the dreaded package tour barbecue. Equally clearly, it has thereby achieved its maximum democratisation. Crayfish eating, once an aristocratic and upper middle class pursuit, has become a universal phenomenon, spilling over into the streets, and one already espies a certain contempt for "dumbing down and profanation of fine old customs" on the part of more highbrow, self-appointed guardians of our common heritage.

FILLET OF PLAICE

marinated in lemon, tomato and basil

Serves 4

INGREDIENTS:
8 fillets of plaice
2 lemons
2 tomatoes
5 or 6 leaves of fresh basil
1 fresh clove of garlic
salt, pepper

PROCEDURE:
1. Even if you have shopped the fillets, start by making sure that all the skin has been removed. Squeeze all the juice out of the lemons and then put the fillets in it. Leave them for at least four hours.
2. Peel the tomato. The easiest way is by making a slit in the bottom of each one and then dipping them in boiling water for 30 seconds. After peeling them, crush them in a food processor before adding the basil leaves and the clove of garlic. Add salt and pepper to taste.
3. When the fillets have been in the lemon juice long enough, transfer them to the tomato mixture.
4. To serve, put the fish on a plate, garnish with one or two fresh basil leaves and serve as a starter. A slice of coarse bread makes a good accompaniment.

COOK'S COMMENT

This composition was inspired by the South American dish "ceviche". A pleasant variant, with a clear affinity to our pickled herring. This isn't a very Scanian composition, lemons being rather a foreign touch, but if only we'd had lemons growing here, I'm sure the people of Skåne would have appreciated this dish every bit as much as their beloved herring.

FROTHY MUSSEL SOUP WITH POLLACK (WHITING)

Serves 4

INGREDIENTS:

1/2 onion
40 blue mussels
3 dl white wine
1/2–1 dl mussel or fish stock
5 dl milk
5 dl double cream
salt, pepper
400 g pollack

PROCEDURE:

1. Chop the onion very small.
2. Rinse and scrub the mussels really thoroughly. Boil them in water for about five minutes or until they have opened. Discard the bad ones – the ones that don't open.
3. Bring the wine to the boil together with the chopped onions. Add the stock, milk and cream, with salt and pepper to taste.
4. Mix some of the mussels (without their shells) and the soup in a mixer or food processor. Return the soup to the saucepan.
5. Cut up the fish in small pieces.
6. Bring the soup to the boil again, put in the mussels and pieces of fish and heat the soup thoroughly, to make sure the pieces of fish are properly cooked.

Serve instantly.

SALAD OF BEANS, ONION AND POTATO WITH SHELLFISH

on white bread and blue cheese au gratin

4 sandwiches

INGREDIENTS:
25 g wax beans
25 g string beans
25 g mangetout
25 g broad beans
1/2 red onion
4 potatoes, boiled and sliced
100 g blue cheese
4 slices white bread
1/2 dl balsamic vinegar
1 dl rape seed oil or olive oil
salt and pepper
shellfish: if possible, various kinds, such as mussels, shrimps, crab, crayfish (quantities according to taste and length of pocket)

PROCEDURE:
1. Prepare all the shellfish. Boil the mussels, shell the shrimps, crayfish etc.
2. Shell the broad beans and boil them in salted water for 1–2 minutes.
3. Slice the onion.
4. Mix all the beans and shellfish with the sliced potato and onion to make a salad, and distribute this on the slices of bread.
5. Top with a little blue cheese and gratinate in the oven, using top heat only, 175°C for 3–5 minutes.
6. Meanwhile shake a vinaigrette sauce of balsamic vinegar, rape seed/ olive oil and a little salt and pepper.
7. When the cheese has turned a nice colour, remove the sandwiches, transfer them to separate plates, drizzle with some of the vinaigrette and serve.

CRAYFISH CREAM IN A GRAVLAX RING

with crayfish tails and toast

Serves 4

INGREDIENTS:

- 1 side of gravlax (or else cold-smoked salmon)
- about 30 crayfish tails (6–8 per person) peeled and boiled
- 1/2 dl white wine
- 3 egg yolks
- 2–3 tbsp. shellfish stock (alternatively fish stock + tomato purée)
- 1 leaf gelatine
- salt, pepper

PROCEDURE:

For this recipe you need four small ramekins, 2–3 cm high and about 5 cm across.

1. Put the yolks in a stainless saucepan with the wine and the stock, whisk over a gentle flame, or perhaps over a bain-marie, till you get a fluffy consistency. (Rather like a béarnaise sauce.) Salt and pepper to taste.
2. Put the gelatine to soak in a bowl of cold water. Wring it out and add it to the egg yolk mixture. Stir until dissolved.
3. Put 3–4 crayfish tails in each ramekin, pour on the egg yolk mixture, then leave to cool in the fridge about an hour.
4. Meanwhile, cut fairly thin slices of the salmon. Each slice should be about 2–3 cm wide.
5. Remove the ramekins from the fridge and tip out the contents. Wind a slice of salmon round the crayfish cream, which by now will have set, and transfer to a plate. It is a good idea to serve this on a bed of lettuce, with the surplus crayfish tails as a surrounding garnish. A good vinaigrette, preferably a little on the sweet side, will enhance the flavour, and a little toast is also a nice added touch.

CRAYFISH SALAD

with an "orgy" of fresh herbs, strawberries and blueberries

Serves 4

INGREDIENTS:
20–30 crayfish
3–4 pots or bunches of fresh (soft) herbs of every kind (though not rosemary, which can be a little too hard)
1 l. strawberries
1/2 l. blueberries

CRAYFISH STOCK
5–10 heads of dill
1/2 onion, sliced
1–11/2 l. small beer
water
2–3 tbsp. salt

PROCEDURE:
The crayfish can very well be cooked a day in advance. (N.B. They should first be killed by putting them in boiling hot water. To avoid unnecessary suffering, don't put in too many at a time.)
1. Make a stock of heads of dill, half an onion, and equal parts of small beer and water, heavily salted. Boil for 15 or 20 minutes.
2. Put the crayfish in the stock and boil for 5 or 6 minutes. Leave the crayfish cool, immersed in the stock, in the fridge overnight.
3. Shell the crayfish and arrange a salad using only fresh herbs, berries and crayfish tails.
Expensive? Yes, and worth every penny!

COOK'S COMMENT

You can afford to be extravagant with crayfish left over from a crayfish party. Every self-respecting castle and manor house in Skåne had its own crayfish waters, so there is a tradition here. One of the many distinguishing features of the Scanian kitchen has been spicier flavours compared with further north. This was mainly because herbs were used. Be lavish with these and you will get a top-flight salad.

MONKFISH BAKED IN BEETROOT LEAVES

with potato purée baked in root vegetables and a beetroot butter sauce

Serves 4

INGREDIENTS:

1 kg potatoes (not new)
1/2 kg fresh beetroot with the tops left on
2 large carrots
2 large parsnips
1/2 kg butter
2 dl milk
salt, pepper
1 leek
800 g fillet of monkfish
1 shallot
1 dl white wine

PROCEDURE:

For this recipe you need a ring about 5 cm high and 1 dm across.

1. Peel the potatoes and all the root vegetables and reserve the beetroot leaves, rinsing them well.
2. Boil the potatoes.
3. Cut the beetroot into segments, using another saucepan, boil them in slightly salted water for about 5 minutes. Put them to one side, still in their liquid.
4. When the potatoes are ready, mash them with 100 g butter. Pour on the milk and carry on whisking until the mixture thickens again. Add salt and pepper to taste.
5. Slice the carrots, parsnips and blanche them (boil slightly) in lightly salted water.
6. Cut the green part of the leek into long strips and blanche these as well.
7. Put the ring in a roasting tin. Place some of the sliced carrots and parsnips on the outer edge. Fill in with mashed potato. Remove the ring.
8. Tie a strip of leek round this roundel so that it holds together. Repeat the procedure until you have enough roundels of root vegetables and mashed potato (at least one per person).
9. Using a cheese slice, cut one slice of butter to put on each of the roundels. Scatter a little salt on each one as well.
10. Cut the fish into 4 portions and add a little salt. Pack it in the beetroot leaves and bake in the oven at 100°C for 5 minutes. Turn off the oven and leave for another 5 minutes.
11. Bake the potato rounds as well for about 5 minutes or until they are a nice colour.
12. Peel and chop the shallot and fry it slightly in a knob of butter.
13. Pour on the wine, reduce slightly or wait until it starts to thicken, and then add the rest of the butter, at room temperature, a knob at a time, stirring continuously. Keep stirring until you have a smooth sauce. Add a little of the beetroot liquor, to give the sauce a nice colour. Add salt and pepper to taste.
14. For each guest, serve one monkfish package, a potato roundel and a few pieces of beetroot together with the sauce, which is as good as it is beautiful.

PIKE-PERCH BAKED IN MARJORAM

in open, fresh cabbage leaves
with a salad of radish, apple and red onion in mayonnaise

Serves 4

INGREDIENTS:
1 dl cooking oil
1 pot of marjoram or 2–3 pinches of the dried version
salt
800 g pike-perch fillet (preferably scaled but with the skin left on)
8–10 radishes
2 apples, de-cored
1/2 red onion
1 summer-fresh head of (white) cabbage

MAYONNAISE:
1 dl cooking oil
2 egg yolks
1 tsp. mustard
1 tbsp. white wine vinegar
salt, pepper
or about 2 dl ready-made mayonnaise

PROCEDURE:
For this recipe you need a mixer or food processor.
1. Begin by pouring 1 dl oil into the mixer together with marjoram and a pinch of salt. Mix to a smooth green oil.
2. Divide the fish into pieces of the preferred size, scatter with a little salt and transfer to an oven-proof dish.
3. Pour on the green marjoram oil. Bake in the oven at 67–70°C for about 30 minutes or until the fish is ready. (If you bake the fish this slowly, all the proteins will be retained, making it both lovelier and more nourishing.)
4. Meantime, rinse the radishes, apple and onion and chop them in small pieces.
5. Mix your own mayonnaise by running 1 dl oil, 2 egg yolks, 1 dob of mustard, 1 tbsp. vinegar and a little salt and pepper in a mixer. Mix the mayonnaise with the vegetables and you will have a rémoulade sauce with a bit of difference.
6. Make four small “baskets” out of the cabbage leaves and distribute the fish between them. Put the baskets in the oven and leave them there for the last five minutes.
7. Serve with boiled new potatoes or baked potato and offer the rémoulade sauce.

COOK’S COMMENT

Pike-perch is a wonderful freshwater fish to be caught in many Scanian lakes. I usually get mine from Börringe Lake near Svedala. Göte comes and sells me what he has caught. He has been fishing that lake for over 40 years. Extraordinary giants, weighing anything up to 12 kg. There are few green vegetables that can rival fresh white cabbage for flavour. Ordinary white cabbage tastes good, but the crisp, new version is best.

CAPON FILLET AU GRATIN WITH RHUBARB

with green vegetables stir-fried in tarragon and a rhubarb sauce

Serves 4

INGREDIENTS:
1 kg rhubarb
about 3 dl sugar (more or less if preferred)
1 cucumber
about 10 shallots or other small onions
about 10 radishes
1 pot/bunch of tarragon (or 1–2 pinches of the dried version)
cooking fat for frying
about 1 dl veal stock (depending on strength)
or 1 veal stock cube
salt, pepper
arrowroot or cornflour for thickening
1/2–1 dl dried bread crumbs
4 capon fillets

PROCEDURE:
1. Remove the leaves from the rhubarb, wash and peel it and divide it into pieces 3–5 cm long. Put these in a casserole and cover with plenty of water.
2. Add the sugar and simmer for about 30 minutes or until the rhubarb has turned into a compote. Check the sweetness.
3. Strain the compote, reserving the liquid in a small casserole. Reduce the liquid by simmering for about 10 minutes.
4. Cut the cucumber into strips or rods and the small onions and radishes into segments. Save 1 onion for the sauce.
5. Chop the tarragon slightly.

6. THE SAUCE. Chop the onion fine. Fry slightly in a little fat in the casserole. Pour on the rhubarb stock and veal stock and reduce slightly. Top up with about 1/2 litre water or until you think the sauce is of the right strength. Boil for a while longer before adding salt and pepper to taste.
7. Thicken with arrowroot or cornflour, mixed with a little cold water, to a suitable consistency.
8. Mix the drained rhubarb with 1/2–1 dl bread crumbs to make a proper dough.
9. Put this dough on top of the capon fillets and bake in the oven at 175°C for 15 or 20 minutes or until they are cooked in the middle. (Not too long, though, because otherwise they will go dry. Check by making a slit in the middle of the thickest fillet.)
10. Quickly fry the cucumber, the radishes, onion and tarragon in a fry pan with just a very little fat. Add salt and pepper.
11. Serve the fillets au gratin on top of the vegetables and surrounded by the sauce.

RARE BREAST OF DUCK IN ELDERBERRY SAUCE

Serves 4

INGREDIENTS:
1 carrot
1 parsnip
1/2 celeriac
1/2 onion
fat for frying
2 duck breasts
1–2 bunches of elderberries
1/2 dl red wine
1/2–1 dl veal stock
a little elderberry juice (optional)
1–2 dl water
salt, pepper
arrowroot, cornflour – or potato flour, dissolved in cold water, for thickening
accessories: potatoes, green vegetables, e.g. string beans, baby corn or Brussels sprouts

PROCEDURE:
Prepare some potatoes and green vegetables to serve with it. Baked, raw-fried or chipped potatoes will do fine. A few stir-fried string beans and baby corn or boiled sprouts will also go down well.

1. Peel the root vegetables and onion and chop them small.
2. Warm a frying pan with a little fat in. Brown the duck breasts, salt and pepper them and then remove them from the pan. Wrap them in a little grease-proof paper and finish them off on the after-heat, preferably in a warming oven, if you have one, or else on the hob close to a heat source.
3. Fry the diced root vegetables and onion in a little fat with the elderberries (perhaps saving a few berries for garnish).
4. Pour on the wine, the stock and, if required, a little elderberry juice to heighten the elderberry flavour. Top up with water and bring to the boil.
5. Add salt and pepper to taste, and thicken with the flour to the right consistency.
6. Put out the vegetables on plates or a serving dish. Slice the duck breasts and pour the sauce round or serve it separately. A little elderberry garnish makes a nice extra touch.

MINCED VEAL OLIVES, GREEK STYLE

with Scanian blueberries and lingonberries

Serves 4

INGREDIENTS:
1/2 onion
1 apple
100 g smoked pork
300 g minced veal
1 dl double cream
2 eggs
1 tsp. caraway
salt, pepper
100–200 g sheep's milk cheese (more or less, if preferred)
1 silverskin (white Portugal) onion
1 red onion
1 head pink lettuce
1 box mache lettuce
1 box ruccola lettuce
4 ripe tomatoes
1 dl blueberries
1 dl lingonberries (cowberries)
1 dl cold-pressed rape seed oil
3–5 tbsp. good vinegar

PROCEDURE:
1. Chop the 1/2-onion, apple and smoked pork very small.
2. Mix them with the minced veal, together with the cream and eggs. Fold in the caraway, and salt and pepper to taste.
3. Shape the farce into "sausages" and transfer to an oven-proof dish.
4. Roast in the oven at 100°C for ten minutes. Then turn the oven off and leave them to finish.
5. Dice the sheep's milk cheese, if you haven't bought it ready-diced.
6. Peel and slice the silverskin onion and the red onion. Tear the pink lettuce into strips, slice the tomatoes and rinse the berries.
7. Make a vinaigrette sauce of oil and vinegar. Add salt and pepper to taste, plus any other spices you may fancy.
8. Mix the different lettuces together and put on plates. Distribute the cheese cubes, onion, tomato slices and berries on the lettuce and pour on your tasty vinaigrette.

COOK'S COMMENT

Voilà! A good idea stolen from the Greek kitchen, with a Scanian touch added!

SKÅNE SPICED LEG OF PORK

with a warm salad of whole new potatoes

Serves 4

INGREDIENTS:
1 kg new potatoes (small ones!)
1 dl honey
3 tbsp. concentrated apple juice
1 pinch ground ginger
1 pinch ground cinnamon
1 pinch ground cardamom
1 pinch ground cloves
about 1 kg neck or loin of pork
fat for frying
salt, pepper
1 red onion
1/2 leek
1-2 apples
1 large or 2 small carrots
about 10 radishes
1/2 dl good vinegar

PROCEDURE:
1. Scrub and boil the potatoes.
2. Mix the honey, concentrated apple juice, ginger, cinnamon, cardamom and cloves in a small bowl.
3. Brown the pork in the frying pan with just a little fat, then salt and pepper it.
4. Now brush it with the mixture, transfer to an oven-proof dish and leave in the oven at 175°C for about 20 minutes.
5. Turn off the oven, remove the pork and baste again generously. (Important! Save a little of the honey mixture for the salad.)
6. Wrap the pork in baking tray paper, return it to the oven and roast it for another 15 minutes or until it is done all the way through. (If necessary, turn the oven back on and give it a few more minutes. The exact time will of course depend on the size of your meat.)
7. While waiting for the meat to be done, you might as well prepare all the vegetables for the potato salad.
8. Peel and cut up the red onion. Make a slit all the way down the leek and rinse well before chopping up.
9. Cut the apples in segments and decore them. Leave the peel on.
10. Peel the carrot and chop in small pieces. Rinse the radishes thoroughly.
11. Put the cooking fat in a large frying pan or wok pan and quickly fry all cream vegetables and the potato.
12. Pour on the vinegar and, last of all, the rest of the honey mixture. Serve the potato salad warm or lukewarm with thick slices of the juicy pork.

WILD BOAR AND PEAR STEW, FLAVOURED WITH ELDERBERRY

Serves 4

INGREDIENTS:
1 onion
3 carrots
2 parsnips
1/2 swede
1/2 celeriac
500–600 g diced shoulder of wild boar
fat for frying
2–3 bunches of elderberries
1 dl concentrated elderberry juice
2 pears
salt, pepper

PROCEDURE:
1. Peel the onion and cut into "collops".
2. Peel the root vegetables and divide into suitable pieces.
3. Brown the diced meat in a little fat on a high flame, using a wide saucepan or casserole.
4. Add the root vegetables. Put in half the berries, hulled and rinsed. Pour on the juice and then top up with water until the meat is covered completely.
5. Bring to the boil. Replace the lid and simmer until the meat is tender enough to be divided with an ordinary table knife (30 or 40 minutes).
6. Split and de-core the pears. Dice them with the peel on and put them into the stew with the rest of the berries. Stir and add salt and pepper to taste.
7. Serve the stew with ordinary boiled potatoes. A floury variety, such as King Edward or something similar, is advisable, for mopping up the sauce, which is really yummy.

COOK'S COMMENT

Elderberries aren't used as often as elderflowers, which is a great pity because they add a very good flavour. In this recipe I have given them their chance together with what are considered the humbler parts of the wild boar.

FILLET OF BEEF INTERSPERSED WITH BLACK RADISH AND CARROT

with a creamy sauce of summer chanterelles

Serves 4

INGREDIENTS:
500 g summer chanterelles
1/2 onion
fat for frying
1 dl white wine
2–3 dl crème fraîche
salt, pepper
800 g fillet of beef
1 black radish
1–2 carrots

PROCEDURE:
1. Trim the chanterelles.
2. Chop the half-onion small and fry quickly in a saucepan, using just a little fat. Add the trimmed chanterelles and fry everything together for a minute or two.
3. Pour on the wine and cook until it is almost completely absorbed.
4. Pour on the crème fraîche and 2–3 tsp. water. Reduce. Add salt and pepper to taste. Put the sauce to one side.
5. Remove any sinews and any "tab" at the top of the fillet of beef. Trim the tab as well.
6. Brown the fillet quickly in a frying pan, with the cooking fat, at maximum heat. Remove the meat, salt and pepper it and then wrap it in greaseproof paper and just a little aluminium foil.
7. Finish off the meat in a low oven, 50-70°C, for 1/2–1 hour. The estimated inside temperature for rare meat is 60°C and for more well-done 65–70°C. A meat thermometer is very useful, except that there will then be a small hole in the slices of meat when you come to serve them.
8. Peel the root vegetables and slice into "pennies". Blanch/stir-fry or boil them lightly.
9. Heat the sauce and carve the meat.
10. Serve alternate layers of meat and root vegetables. For good measure, you can put an extra layer of root vegetables under the meat. They deserve it!

BEEF STEAK WITH ONION ON "MADA" FRIED IN RAPE-SEED OIL

with a lean green vegetable "Béarnaise" and roast pommes château

Serves 4

INGREDIENTS:
600–700 chuck or rump
3 carrots
6 potatoes for baking
cold-pressed rape-seed oil
salt, pepper
2 dl green peas
1 onion
1 red onion
cooking fat for frying
4 slices of bread

PROCEDURE:
For this recipe you need a mixer or food processor.
1. Trim away all sinews and membranes from the beef before cutting it into four slices of equal thickness.
2. Peel the carrots, wash the potatoes thoroughly. Cut the potatoes into wedges and put these in a roasting tin. Brush with a little oil and salt. Roast in the oven at 175°C for about 30 minutes or until the wedges are a beautiful golden brown and start to "bubble".
3. Cut the carrots into small pieces and boil them in salt water in a saucepan until they are really soft. Then add the peas and let the whole thing go on cooking for a minute or two.
4. Drain the peas and carrots and transfer them to a mixer. Add water, if necessary, for a "saucier" consistency. Add salt and pepper to taste.
5. Peel and slice the onion and fry it until soft in a little rape-seed oil in a frying pan.
6. Fry the beef on a high flame in a knob of cooking fat, to seal it. Remove, wrap in a little grease-proof paper, and return to the pan to finish cooking in its own heat.
7. Last of all, fry the slices of bread in a little rape-seed oil in the frying pan.
8. Put one slice of fried bread in each plate. Put the beef on this and a little fried onion on the beef. Pour the sauce all round and serve with the pommes château. A tolerably lean version of a 1970s classic.

STRAWBERRY FRITTERS

with sweet sherry sauce, vanilla ice cream and a quick and easy strawberry ice cream

Serves 4–8

INGREDIENTS:

1 l. fresh frozen strawberries + 20 fresh ones for garnish
1 1/2 dl sugar
2 dl milk yoghurt natural
10 sheets of filo pastry
1 egg for brushing
2 dl sweet sherry
arrowroot or cornflour for thickening
3 dl double cream
1 vanilla pod

PROCEDURE:

For this recipe you need a mixer and a casserole with a frying basket (or else a big, deep casserole, half-filled with cooking oil) and a great deal of care.

1. Start by getting out 1 l. fresh-frozen strawberries, so that they will have time to thaw out a little. Run them to a smooth paste in a mixer. Add 1/2 dl sugar and yoghurt and mix again. Pour the mixture into a mould or basin and put it in the freezer.
2. Get out the filo pastry sheets. Divide each one in two (or perhaps four, depending on size).
3. Put one strawberry on each filo piece. Brush round with egg and fold as tightly as possible, to exclude air pockets.
4. Bring the sherry to the boil with 1/2 dl sugar and thicken with the flour to a heavy consistency.
5. Pour the double cream into a basin. Split the vanilla pod down the middle and scrape the contents into the cream. Add about 1/2 dl sugar (more or less, according to taste) and whisk the cream stiff.
6. Keep the oil in the frying basket/casserole. When deep frying in a casserole on the hob, remember to have a few towels handy. And remember NOT to use water if the oil starts to burn. (If it starts to burn just on the hob, all you really need to do is let it burn out. It will soon die down.)
7. Deep-fry the strawberry packets 5 or 6 at a time, without overcrowding the casserole. Fry them until they are a lovely golden colour. It will take 2 or 3 minutes.
8. Serve the fritters immediately with some yoghurt ice cream, sherry sauce and a dob of vanilla cream.

SWEET TARRAGON CREAM BETWEEN TARRAGON-FLAVOURED CHOCOLATE SNAPS

and a heavily reduced cherry sauce

Serves 4

INGREDIENTS:

1 pot/bunch of fresh tarragon
5 dl crème fraîche
1 dl sugar
2 egg yolks
100 g dark cooking chocolate
1/2 kg stoneless cherries

PROCEDURE:

For this recipe you need a mixer or a food processor.

1. Run about half the tarragon in the mixer together with 1/2 dl water, to make a green liquid.
2. Whisk the crème fraîche, 1/2 dl sugar and egg yolks to a firm consistency before folding in some of the green tarragon liquid.
3. Put the remaining liquid through a very fine strainer or strain through a cloth.
4. Melt the chocolate and when it is melted, mix in some of the green paste. Now pour out the chocolate mixture onto grease-proof paper to firm cakes 7–8 cm in diameter. You should get at least 2 cakes per person (8 in all).
5. Put tarragon leaves on top of the cakes and then leave in the fridge to set for about 10 minutes. Remove from the fridge at the end of that time, so that the cakes will not "perspire".
6. For each dessert, put two chocolate snaps together with tarragon cream in between.

CHERRY SAUCE:

Run the cherries in the mixer with 1/2 dl sugar.

VANILLA MOUSSE

with red currants and elderberry-flavoured rhubarb soup

Serves 4

INGREDIENTS:

VANILLA MOUSSE:
1 vanilla pod
2 1/2 dl double cream
2 1/2 dl milk
1/2 dl sugar
3 leaves of gelatine

ELDERBERRY/RHUBARB SOUP:
1 stick of rhubarb
1 dl concentrated elderberry juice
2 dl sugar
garnish: 2–3 bunches of red currants

PROCEDURE:
1. Split the vanilla pod down the middle and scrape the seeds into a saucepan. Put in the pod as well.
2. Add the cream, milk and sugar, mix and bring to the boil. Remove the vanilla pod.
3. Dissolve the gelatine leaves in a little cold water. Wring them out and put them in the warm vanilla cream. Stir until completely dissolved.
4. Pour the mousse into coffee cups or suchlike and chill thoroughly in the fridge.
5. Scrape or peel the rhubarb and chop.
6. Boil the pieces of rhubarb with the concentrated juice, sugar and 1 dl water for about 5 minutes. Add sugar to taste, or else more water.
7. Serve the mousse, when it has set completely. Run a knife round the edge of it, so that the mousse comes away from the side, then turn it out onto a plate and serve with the elderberry-rhubarb soup. Garnish with red currants.

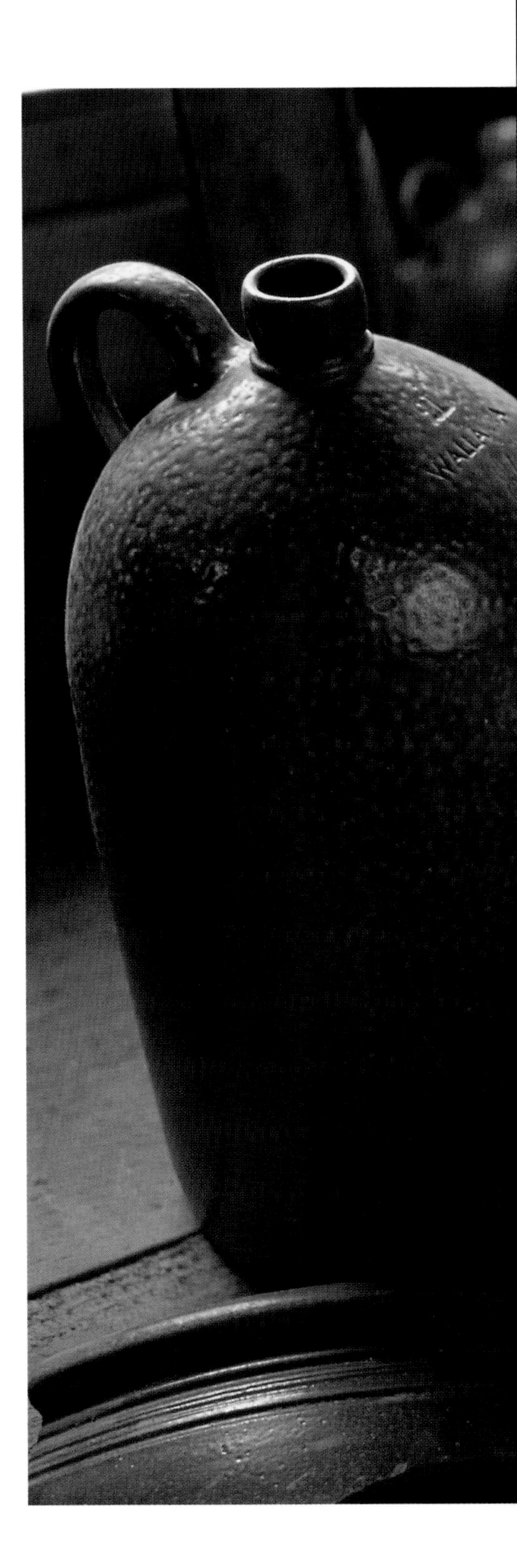

Scanian stoneware

The Swedish stoneware industry was born in north-western Skåne and is still going strong there. Stoneware is as much a part of Skåne as glassware of Småland. "Industry" is rather a misleading word, because this is and remains a craft which no machine can take over.

One firm that is still thriving is Wallåkra Stenkärlsfabrik, a little way south-east of Helsingborg. This is one of the six factories that were founded in the mid-18th century onwards. There is one main reason why they are so thick on the ground here: the clay. But we have coal-mining to thank for the clay being brought to light, because to get at the coal they had to dig up the clay first. And once the clay had been dug up, it might as well be used for something.

The founder of the Swedish stoneware industry was Anton Swab, a partner in the Skånska Stenkolsverket coal company. He started the Bosarp

Potters at their wheels under the foreman's watchful eye at Kärlfabriken, Höganäsbolaget. Photo: Peter P. Lundh, c. 1900.

stoneware factory, using a special firing and salt-glazing technique developed in Germany. Nothing survives of the factory's output, but the technique today is still that introduced by Anton Swab.

The coal-fired round kiln at Wallåkra stoneware factory is constructed just like the kilns of the 18th century.

From outside it resembles a huge igloo, made of beautiful fired brick with enormous hoops to keep the walls of the kiln from expanding from the tremendous heat. Vessels are fired at a temperature of 1,300°C, and it takes nearly three days intensive stoking through the seven stoke holes to reach this temperature. But there are a good many things that have to be done first.

The clay for stoneware is obtained on site. It is slurried in wooden troughs, strained and stored. Meanwhile it is turned by hand and then wedged and kneaded to the right consistency. Then and only then is it time for "throwing". Everything is done by hand and the only element of mechanisation is a few benchmarks, mostly for vessels sizes. And experienced hands use them more as a check than as a template.

Once the vessels have been raised they are put out to dry, slowly. As the stock for drying accumulates, the kiln is fitted with shelving on which the

vessels are gradually installed, on clay dishes. Inside the kiln is more than four metres in diameter and more than the height of a man. It is methodically filled with the dried vessels and when it is full right up the door is closed and firing can commence.

It takes seven tons of coal to raise the right temperature. The heat rises to the dome of the kiln, but the flue gas channel at the bottom of the oven distributes the heat to every corner. At the critical temperature the pots are glazed by throwing salt in through the stoke holes. This gasifies and somehow combines with the high-temperature fired clay. Timing is of the essence, and the critical interval is little more than an hour long.

The clay sinters, which makes it as hard as stone and endows the stoneware with its unique quality of not absorbing any liquid. This is the quality which has made stoneware pots such popular storage vessels for several hundred years now.

After salt-glazing, the kiln is allowed to cool and, just over a week later, the door can be re-opened and the finished pots removed. Due to the process taking such a long time, the factory cannot manage more than four, perhaps five, firings a year. But some things can't be rushed, thank goodness.

A U T U M N

In autumn I die every time

In autumn I die every time
but no one bothers to bury me.

In winter I come to life when
everything freezes, and I tinkle a bit
when rising on a kite string.

In spring I start humming in the middle of the day
dilating in strange songs
and it is the dandelions that lift the roof line
of the sky and have me twittering with the thrushes.

In summer when somebody calls my name
the cuckoo answers instead of me. When I shout back
the marlpit greenhouses answer where there is creeping
and crawling, swimming and diving, flowering
and withering: Be our guest.

CARL MAGNUS VON SETH

From "Märgelgraven", 1992

Autumn. Time of harvest and preservation

Autumn is harvest time. So it used to be in the society of yesteryear, and so it is today. Harvest festivals, with fresh root vegetables, magnificent marrows and pumpkins and newly slaughtered lamb and game, spread through the land. This is a manifestation whose history goes deep, for example by way of harvest festival services in church, and it is worth preserving and developing.

In the old days, by which I mean above all before the coming of modern preserving methods in the first half of the 20th century, the proceeds of harvesting had to be eked out all the year round. The corn was cut and threshed, lambs, calves and yearling pigs were slaughtered, and the fruits of sea and forest had to be preserved for the lean months ahead. In addition, of course, the fruits of the harvest were the stuff of which festivals were made, but more about that later.

One of the oldest preservation methods is *drying*. Above all it was fish that was dried, but sometimes meat as well. Fish were opened and gutted and then a withy or a string passed through them for hanging up. Often this kind of drying took place out of doors on special racks. Sometimes too, gutted fish was hung straight on the wall of the house, in the direction of the prevailing wind. From Väsby we have the following description: "In summer, Mother would buy large flatfish. These would be gutted and cut straight across, after which their tails would be tied together with yarn and they would be

"Threshing Rape. Skåne, 1858." Painting by Wilhelm Wallander.

Back from the hunt. Skurup, 1920s.

hung on a line to dry in the wind. Once dried, they could be put away for winter."

Meat and sausage, unlike fish, needed warmth for drying. So they were often dried in the sauna or in the malt kiln, which was a small building heated from a stove and, because of the fire risk, often situated a distance from the other farm buildings.

As a preserving method, drying in Skåne-style oast houses rather resembles *smoking*. Smoking is also a very ancient means of prolonging the useful life of foodstuffs, and it has been practised almost nationwide. In the extreme south of Sweden, the food to be smoked was simply nailed up in the big chimney of the dwelling house. Meat or fish was often lightly salted before smoking. For good results, broadleaf wood (alder preferably) and juniper were used as fuel. A combination of smoking and drying was commonly used for both meat and fish.

Most households would only slaughter livestock once or twice a year. Whatever was preserved in the autumn would have to last a good many months before stocks could be replenished. An old saying had it that "spike ham", meaning the meat that was nailed up to dry in autumn, must not be eaten until the cuckoo had been heard in the early summer. From the north-east of Skåne we are told that "we made spike meat at the Christmas slaughtering, and so it was hung up at Christmas and there it stayed. Mother hung it in the living room and then, when they'd heard the spike meat bird for the first time, it was ready for cutting." Today perhaps herring and eel are the first things to come to mind on the subject of smoking in Skåne. In Österlen especially, smoke-houses sprang up already in the 19th century, selling finished products to people living round about. And show me the visitor to, say, Kåseberga who can leave without a few smoked herring.

Fermentation and "graving" also belong to the most ancient preserving methods. Originally, whatever had to be preserved was buried in a stone-lined pit (hence the expression gravlax). This was topped with thin, flat stones and, uppermost, a layer of soil. Then the whole thing was left to ferment. All over Northern Europe and Asia, foodstuffs were preserved in this way, and in Iceland especially the method is very much alive today. Gravlax and fermented herring (surströmming) were originally produced this way.

Unquestionably, the most persistent and widely used of the ancient preserving method is *salting*. Sweden

Herring on sale at Norra Vallgatan, Malmö, 1917.

doesn't have any salt mines, and so all salt had to be imported. This made it expensive, because it had to be bought for cash. We do not know how long salt has been used for preserving, but, no matter how expensive, it has been pretty common since medieval times, especially in the south of Sweden. The further north one went, the more expensive salt became, as witness the salt cellars of Norrland (northern Sweden). These are small and exquisitely crafted, clearly intended as receptacles for a costly product, in contrast to the much bigger and more rough-and-ready ones used in Skåne. Then again, Scanian food has always been saltier than food in other parts of Sweden. Both meat and fish were salted down, but salt herring was most important of all. The herring to be salted was obtained during the autumn, either from travelling herring mongers or directly from the coastal fishermen - unless, of course, you did your own fishing. A Jonstorp housewife remembers: "Every household salted down herrings. Even a small family would salt down 15 or 20 *valar* – well over a thousand. Sometime or other during the day you always had herring." But salting called for one or two dodges. As a woman from Höör explains: "We would leave the pork in salt six weeks. If you sprinkled a little white pepper over it now and then, you wouldn't have any trouble with pinworms. Their favourite place was by the bone in the middle of the ham, unless you powdered it with white pepper during the salting. They didn't like white pepper at all, so that got rid of them."

Fishing for herring in Öresund. From Olaus Magnus' History of the Nordic Peoples. 1555.

Even milk was "preserved", because fresh milk was rarely to be seen on the farmer's table. Very young children and old people drank it as a kind of medicine, but hardly anyone else. The main method of preserving milk was by turning it into butter or cheese.

The butter was churned with the fat cream skimmed from the milk. There were two principal ways of making cheese, namely with or without the coagulant rennet. Cheese-

Dairymaids at Näsbygård, Skurup, 1910s.

Delivering churns of milk, Tommarp, 1920s.

making without rennet, the oldest method, required the addition of fermented milk.

Syltemjölk, a regional speciality of south-western Skåne, was sheep's milk which had been boiled and salted and then left in a bowl to ferment. This had to be stirred every day. It grew steadily thicker and after just over a week it was ready. *Syltemjölk* was served in a communal bowl, and the following record from Vemmenhög explains how it was eaten. "Each one cut his bread in pieces which were impaled on the point of the knife, and then you dipped one side of the bread in the bowl. You weren't allowed to dip it right in, that would have been both rude and extravagant."

Fruit and vegetables required their own preserving methods. It has to be said, though, that the Swedes have never been big eaters of green vegetables or fruit, at all events compared with people further south in Europe. Cucumber, beetroot, carrots and peas, then, came relatively late to Everyman's table in this country. In most instances the path to our daily table went by way of the monasteries and castle and manor house gardens.

Cabbage, though, is an ancient vegetable, especially in Skåne. Green Scandinavian cabbage needed hardly any preserving at all, because it could be left unharvested all winter. One old method of preserving white cabbage, and other green vegetables

too, is lactic acid fermentation. The foodstuffs to be fermented are cut in small pieces and lightly salted, preferably using sea salt. The food is then put in a wooden, stoneware or glass vessel and left to self-ferment. The best methods are those with some kind of water lock, so that the carbon monoxide formed during fermentation would escape without atmospheric oxygen being able to enter. The sauerkraut which is still so common, for example, in Germany and Austria, is fermented in this way.

Fruit, and green vegetables too, could also be preserved by boiling in bottles or jars. The food to be preserved was put in bottles of water which were brought to the boil in a bath and then sealed with resin. Afterwards the bottles would be stored in a cold cellar. Fruit could also be dried. Apples in particular were sliced and put in the oven after bread-making or on top of it, on a special drying shelf. Dried fruit was mainly used for fruit soup, which, for a treat was occasionally sweetened with treacle or sugar. The same drying method was used for rosehips in late autumn. Boiling in syrup was another common preserving method, not forgetting squash and jam-making, of course.

The full responsibility of keeping body and soul together until next harvest devolved on the housewife. She was in charge of the larder, cooking and other household chores, and it was her skill and thrift that decided whether the family was in thin time of it during the run-up to spring or whether there would be enough corn and meat to tide them over till the next harvest. Although officially the woman had a subordinate position in earlier society, her duties were important enough. As a housewife from Höganäs puts it: "You had to be content with what you were given. Times weren't easy for housewives either. Without the jar of herring and the pork in the salt trough to rely on, life could be pretty difficult."

Squash and jam store. Notice the decoratively cut paper lining the shelves.

The art of smoking meat – still going strong

Meat-smoking today is an industrialised and centralised process over long distances – from farm to abattoir and smoke-house, and from smoke-house to shop and consumer. Not very long ago, however, things were quite different.

In the 1930s there were plenty of smoke-houses on the Scanian plain. Every abattoir smoked its own meat, and there were two in Genarp, two in Veberöd, two in Dalby and so on. Village upon village had its own abattoir and smoke-house combined. These handled livestock from nearby farms and then sold their products, quite often through shops of their own in the nearest sizeable community. At most a couple of hours away by horse and cart.

Meanwhile, co-operative abattoirs were coming on the scene. The Scanian one had facilities in Kävlinge and Tomelilla, while other co-operatives ran the Malmö abattoir and the big one in Eslöv. The Malmö abattoir was eventually taken over by the co-operative movement (KF), and the Eslöv abattoir was run by the Nilsson brothers.

Meat was smoked to keep it edible.

One of the few surviving practitioners of the art. Tasting is believing, and age tells!

The alternative was to salt it down. For fresh meat you went to the butcher's. Unless you fancied chicken, of course, because that was most often available nearer home.

The usual thing was to slaughter and smoke a pig or two at Christmas and again at Easter. That had to do. Each pig provided two hams, two sides and two shoulders for smoking. In addition, the abattoir would smoke the farmer's own sausages. They were most often made to such a fine recipe that they would keep for anything up to six months.

Part of the secret of long durability was the method used for storing smoked meat and sausages. The ideal storage place was in the loft, especially if your house had a thatched roof, because that way the temperature was kept down during summer and moisture was trapped by the thatch during autumn, winter and spring. If you were really particular you would put the ham in a jute sack, because otherwise one fly could ruin the whole thing.

After a few decades the big abattoirs gradually cornered the market, and the small ones and the smoke-houses are now a thing of the past. There are just a handful of people left who are still versed in the art of smoking meat.

The difference is more than just romantic or academic. The old way of smoking meat has a completely different approach to the raw material from that favoured by the big companies.

First of all, in big plants the heat is generated with LPG or electricity, and to shorten the process times, many firms inject smoke-flavouring agents into the meat, which means they can make do with a superficial, hasty smoking operation.

Hand-crafted smoking is quite different and has quite different input values. Every piece or sausage to be smoked is individually assessed and then put in the oven in a particular order. For cold smoking, the fire is lit with alder and beech chips, with a little juniper wood added. This last mentioned is a matter of taste. Many people use nothing but alder and beech chips. The fire is lit in one corner of the oven, and every morning the smoker inspects the meat and sausage, to decide what is to be taken out and what is to be re-hung.

The best thing is an oven with a completely open chimney, because you need air for good results. For domestic smoking the ordinary fireplace was often used, and it was also used for boiling water and heating the bread ovens. Food for smoking could then be hung over the hearth, in the chimney aperture.

After all its years of service, the inside of the oven is black and shiny. Meat and sausages are moved about in the oven, depending on the raw material, the result aimed for and the current stage in the smoking process. Only the trained eye can tell when the process is complete.

Work and festivities in autumn

Rakers at Svaneholm, Skurup.

First came the hay-making of high summer, then the harvest of early autumn. Both were big enterprises requiring extra manpower in the form of reapers, women rakers and women sheaf-binders. Many people were taken on at the farm, and work occupied every hour of daylight. This heavy work input raised high expectations of good eating. A massive diet was called for, with no lack of either meat or drink. The priest-ethnographer Mattias Solberg tells us that harvesters got through eight meals a day, with generous libations of beer and schnapps. "It is a wonder that they can work and do not get far more drunk than a good many of them are seen to be," he writes, in his description of Söderslätt in the 18th century.

The following description comes from Billeberga. "Everyone who had taken part during the autumn would then foregather... The food was heavy and generous, usually soup made from beef with horseradish sauce, potato and a pudding for afters, and of course schnapps to go with it."

This huge meal was often followed by dancing, accompanied by fiddlers engaged for the occasion. Presumably the hay barn – as yet empty – had been decorated with foliage for the purpose, or else people danced out of doors. Stories of spell-binding fiddlers, the power of music and the allure of the Water Sprite are often associated with harvest festivities of this kind.

The bounty of the soil was sometimes celebrated in rites which if anything are perhaps risqué allusions to hopes for later on that night. From Skanör, for example, we are told that the last sheaves were tied in male and female shapes, with pistils and curvaceous figures being brought together in the last sheaves of the year, to speed the fertility of the next one.

Perhaps the hired labourers were paid a modest wage, but otherwise real payment was the great feast in acknowledgement of work well done.

"Harvest Home Celebration in Skåne." Watercolour by Kilian Zoll (1818–1860).

St Michael's

It has to be said that autumn was not only a time of useful toil and festivities. The 19th century was a period of rapid population growth, resulting in a large number of people being pushed out onto the social and geographic margins of village life as "beach sitters" (fisherfolk), crofters and, eventually, bondagers. The landless population grew, and with it the difference between master and servant. In Skåne it became common practice, in emulation of manor houses and vicarages, for the farm workers to live and eat separately from the farmer and his family.

St Michael's was by tradition "flit day", when farm workers could change masters and when they collected their annual wages. In addition, the farmer's wife had to provide the servants with food (a loaf of bread, a leg of mutton, a piece of pork) for one week ahead. The harvest had been gathered in, and the lads and lasses were given a week off in which to recuperate and look for new positions. Perhaps they would be better off in a new place - many felt that they couldn't possibly be worse off.

The feast of St Michael came on 29th September (the "flit day" was later changed to 24th October). Winter was now in the offing, and candles would be lighted indoors of an evening. This was also the day for weather-forecasting. A strong wind on St Michael's day, for example, augured a cold, windy winter.

St Michael's was above all known as the time for the long-autumn fair. The Höganäs one is especially renowned. The following description comes from about 1900:

"St Michael's Fair was a big day, a real festival, you might say. Dealers came from Dalarna, Småland and many other provinces. Gypsies, diddicoys and Jews from every corner of the world came to do business in their particular way. Long lines of gewgaws, shooting ranges, magicians, big menageries with lots of different animals, including old Jumbo the elephant. The dealers brought wooden craft objects like salt cellars, tubs, wooden pails and rank upon rank of wooden shoes."

Quite a social occasion, in other words, with plenty of opportunity for getting rid of those wages, eating, drinking and dancing.

A social occasion it may have been, but not always a peaceful one. Replete with food and drink, the farmhands would start abusing each other in terms of local patriotism, and you could nearly always be sure of a good fight when lads from Göinge bumped into lads from the plainland. Further south the Göinge people were rated poor, dull and mean while northerners would tell you that the plainlanders were swanky, fat and stupid. The following tale comes from Stoby, in Western Göinge.

The St Michael's Fair in Höganäs, in the early years of the 20th century.

"A bloke from Göinge on his way down to the plain had a live fox and a squirrel with him in a box. He bumped into one of the locals and showed him the fox. The plain-dweller wondered what sort of animal it could be.

"The Göinge bloke told him it was a sheep-painter. 'If you let him into the sheep fold he'll paint the sheep different colours,' said the lad from Göinge. The plain-dweller bought the fox, paid a lot of money for it and shut it up in the sheep fold. A while afterwards he went back to see what colour the sheep were. When he looked inside he saw some of them had been eaten up and others had been bitten to death and were waiting to be eaten."

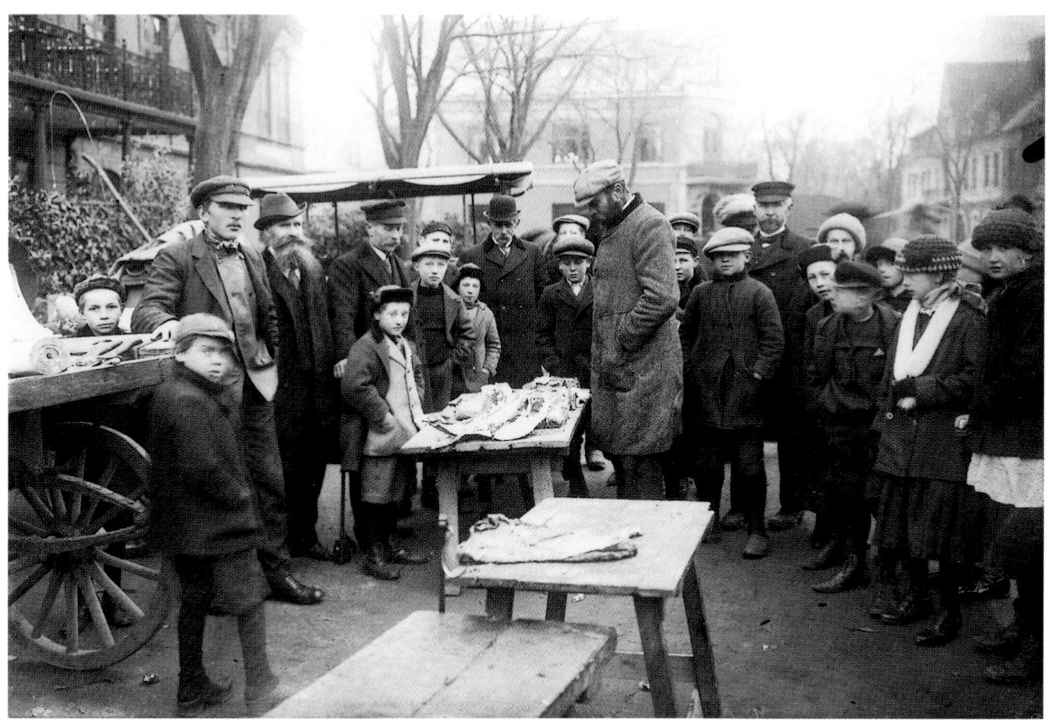

All Hallows

Halloween is a festival lately imported by Sweden from the USA, though its origins are European. In Ireland especially, the end of the summer season and the memory of the departed were and still are celebrated in a special Halloween festival on 31st October. Irish emigrants took the custom with them to America where it has evolved into one of the year's most prominent festivals. Weeks ahead of the actual day, shops begin selling masks representing death's heads, witches or mutilated faces. All this merchandise, costumes included, is meant to make your flesh creep.

Window-dressing focuses on the recently gathered harvest. Pride of place goes to the pumpkins (often cut out to resemble faces and with lanterns inside), in a variety of colours and sizes, but the display also includes sheaves of corn and beautiful autumn leaves. In this way the American version of Halloween is a mixture of harvest festival and All Saints, compared with autumn customs in Sweden.

Halloween has steadily gained popularity in Sweden since the 1990s, though in somewhat modified form. In the USA it is above all adults and youngsters who, on the festival evening, dress up and parade in their variously fantastic and frightening costumes. This sort of thing hardly ever occurs in Sweden – at any rate, yet. Something we have imitated, though, is the children's "Trick or Treat".

Halloween is a good example of the way in which customs migrate and transmogrify but still survive the leap in time and space, which in many ways is a precondition of all cultural transmissions.

All Saints' Day was turned into a double holiday in 1953, to provide an autumnal break. Otherwise it is

spring that seems to have all the holidays. The calendar still gives 1st November as All Saints' Day, recalling a medieval tradition, but that day seldom coincides with the new duplicate holiday. In Catholic times, 2nd November was called All Souls' Day, in memory of the "ordinary" uncanonised departed.

Nowadays All Saints' Day is perhaps above all associated with grave decorations. This is the day when many people put a winter wreath on the grave, and the lighting of lanterns has also been common practice since the mid-20th century.

Eel trap drying, Borrby.

Eel time

Eel time in Österlen is both ancient and modern history. It originated as a kind of confirmation of, and rent for fishing rights, paid by the fishermen to the riparian farmers. The fishermen would treat them to various kinds of eel (boiled, fried, smoked and pickled, for example) and, very often, *sluring* (eel soup), in one of their boathouses, with the farmers supplying the drink.

Otherwise the eel has not always been the delicacy we consider it today. In olden times, many people

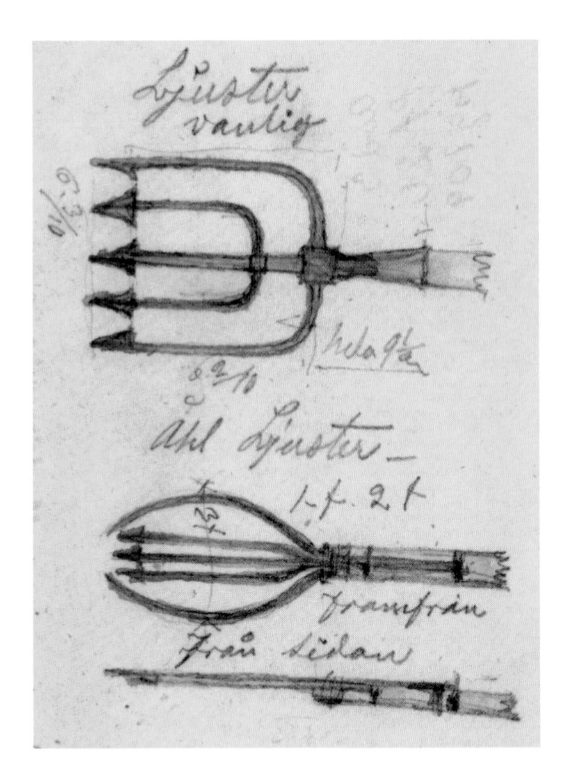

Types of fish-spear. Watercolour by Nils Månsson Mandelgren.

disliked the serpentine fish. They simply didn't know how to classify it. It didn't look the way fish ought to, it was more like the biblical serpent. And anything you couldn't quite pin down was, by definition, suspicious. Added to which, it was believed to live on carrion, especially drowned sailors.

Long line, Östra Göinge. The owner, Nils Svensson, says that fishing up the Immelen is tricky. "You have to put out your long lines in particular places, usually banks and slabs of rock. The troughs you put the line on are like sieves, with just a few slats with ribbons in between for a bottom. Along the edges you saw notches to hold the hooks."

The Bishop's Goose

"Martin Goose" day is unquestionably the biggest gastronomic event of the autumn in Skåne, and away from the province too, roast goose rates as a typical Scanian delicacy.

The origins of *Mårten Gås* are rather complicated. The association of the name with 11th November goes back to the French Bishop Martin of Tours, who died on that day in about 397. Name and day stayed together all through the Middle Ages in the Catholic calendar, and Swedish runic staves show a goose as emblem for the day, not because goose was eaten on this day but rather because it was St Martin's attribute. An explanatory tale has it that Martin once tried to hide in a goose pen but was basely betrayed by the cackling of the inmates.

Goose-herding represents a thousand-year tradition in the plainlands of southern Sweden, and especially in Skåne. The goose provided excellent meat for smoking and drying, down for cushions and quills for writing. The fat was greatly prized for baking and for eating on bread.

Roast goose as we know it from the celebrations of St Martin's Day, though, is a more recent country tradition. In southern Skåne especially the day used above all to be geared to the working year. This was when the village council would meet to appoint a new alderman, and after this day the women were allowed to spin and weave by candlelight in the evenings. Roast goose as festival fare is a middle-class, continental custom associated both with St Martin's and with Christmas – as witness the Christmas goose or duck in Denmark. The custom filtered down to country people (mainly in Skåne) during the second half of the 19th century and early years of the 20th.

There was more to a real St Martin's feast than just roast goose. Fish – stockfish especially – and rice pudding were also part of proceedings, as well as the dessert – apple cake, for example. Eventually, "black soup" also joined the menu.

Martin Goose has also become a signal occasion for Scanian expatriates. Assembling round the festive board, all the way from black soup to apple cake, they swap childhood memories, reminding one another of mutual friends in Skåne, their reminiscences punctuated by the odd drinking song. In this context, the goose is more a Scanian symbol than just food.

Coop for three broody geese.

Geese for sale in the market place. Malmö, 1949–50.

The food of love

Restaurants are a comparatively modern invention, and to get the full picture we must also include pavement cafés, dance restaurants, old-time hostelries and cafés.

They all have one thing in common: music. The food was almost a minor consideration, and the menus were much the same from one establishment to another. Not so the music. In a sense it was through the repertoire that the proprietor attracted his patrons – the bandleaders were the real crowd-pullers – and this too was how the patrons could find congenial company. One went out mainly to listen, not to eat. Cafés and restaurants were meeting points, and you knew exactly in which of them to find a particular person.

Music was already a feature of Malmö's garden cafés in the 1920s. One of the most popular among them was Konditoriträdgården, home of the Johan Åkesson Orchestra – violin, cello, double bass, clarinet and harmonium. Out in the garden alcoves, in addition to the music, you could be served with everything from ice cream to shrimp sandwiches. For a proper meal you could sit down indoors. For every season a repertoire list would be published, containing nearly 1,000 titles, all previously rehearsed and available on request. One of the prime movers here was Trolle Benstedt, to be heard during winter seasons at the Cecil music café on Södergatan. In summertime the Cecil put out a terrace on Södergatan, with its bustling crowds and number one tramcars. In winter there was quasi-jazz from Sven Öberg and his band. Öberg was assisted by "Buck Tooth Adam" on the trumpet, Tönna (bass and vocals) and little brother Klas on the drums. People came here in the thirties and forties to meet friends and listen to music while sipping, at most, a vermouth.

For more concert-like, classical music you could cross the street to the Palladium, which had a café on the second floor. There you could often hear Guido Vecchi, the famous cellist who later joined the Gothenburg Symphony.

Kungsparken had a music pavilion where Mario Galli and his 12- or 14-strong orchestra from the Concert Hall Foundation attracted capacity audiences. They offered both operatic repertoire and music in a lighter vein during warm summer evenings. If you were sitting indoors you would try to get a place by the open windows, so as to hear the music. The menu featured everything from coffee and biscuits to the more sophisticated hot dishes, and the clientèle was much the same as the Cecil's in winter.

Music, of course, wasn't the whole story. There were establishments which were also known for their cuisine. The Savoy, for example, under its legendary chef de cuisine

Pettersson, earned a solid reputation for itself as a temple of gastronomy. The menu – lengthy to say the least of it – included no less than a dozen different versions of sole, as well as a long line of the most wonderful fillet compositions. Black tie was the usual dining garb here in the fifties, and the standard of cooking and social behaviour was kept up for many decades. As an adjunct, the grill was eventually opened on the other side of the entrance, with a slightly different menu by no means inferior in quality to the dining room's. Even so, many would say that the grill's main merits were the bar and the swing doors. But the Savoy also had music, rendered for example by the outstanding violinist Frans Haidl, assisted here by a first-rate bass player and pianist.

In fact all the musicians playing in these restaurants and cafés were top rank. What later became the Malmö Symphony Orchestra had only a short season, and for the rest of the year the players had to fend for themselves. Frans Haidl and the Savoy went in for standard classical tunes, perhaps one or two numbers from a popular musical but never a sound from the hit parade.

The big contest was – and to some extent still is – between the Savoy and the Kramer. The Christmas table was the main battlefield. Capture that public and you were the uncrowned king of the Malmö restaurants. For a long time the Savoy was the obvious choice, but Mr Roodey refused to give in and for a time it was the Kramer which set the tone of pre-Christmas banqueting. The Kramer had a cuisine to rival the Savoy's but in addition to music it also had floor shows. The place went downhill after Roodey died, and the Savoy regained the ascendancy.

After Frans Haidl's classical period, Ferry Racz took over at the Savoy. In addition to being a gifted musician, he had an unbeatable talent for getting the pitch of the hall and varying the repertoire accordingly.

Going out to restaurants remained for a long time a man's activity, with corporate entertainment providing 80 or 90 per cent of the patrons. And reasons for celebration were not lacking. The Kockum shipyard had a steady succession of new ships coming off the stocks, and the racecourse people kept the money spinning as well.

Other famous haunts were the Fenix, Kvarnen and Druvan, this last mentioned in Engelbrektsgatan. Druvan ("The Grape") had a second class restaurant on the upper floor and a third class one downstairs. Service in the latter was unutterably slow, which many people remember but none can explain. The Fenix, Kvarnen and Druvan had few if any culinary ambitions, but a fairly heroic turnover in strong drink. The Sturehof in the 1940s served "two whites and a brown" with a fairly plain menu which included open sandwiches, boeuf à la Lindström, omelettes, beef steak and onions etc. Its present reputation as a first-class fish restaurant was born in the 1960s.

For ten öre the ferry would take you across the harbour inlet to the charming, low-slung Harbour Pavilion on the pier. Åkesson used to play here as well, to an audience midway between those of the Savoy and Sturehof. This place took its food quite seriously.

One of the Malmö classics is Olgas Krog – Olga's Café in those days. Olga was the legendary Olga Hellquist, the sister of Calle, who conducted the Folkets Hus Theatre orchestra, and Anders, a leading figure in the entertainment world and proprietor, for example, of the Stranden restaurant in Limhamn. Olga's Café was next to the open-air theatre which faced the hospital and featured all the big names at that time. Nils Poppe and Edvard Persson performed here, and, not least, Gunnar Björnstrand, at the beginning of his career. The murmur of voices from the tables was accompanied by Areira Tönnes' Orchestra, one of the very best in Sweden. In between

At Amiralen you dined one floor up, "on the shelf". If you weren't fully occupied with each other, you could always watch people dancing down below, on this occasion to the music of Harry Arnold's Orchestra.

ARENA

Regementsgatan 52.

I dag **THE DANSANTE** 3—6.

Fri entré.

DANS 7—12.

Gösta Tönnes

med sin eminenta orkester.

På friluftsscenen kl. 5 och 10,20

2 ARVINGS

cykelspänst i det blå.

Entré 25 öre. Bordbest. 14048.

there was a piano duo playing hits of a more light-hearted nature, and occasionally there was piano music with no dancing.

The Arena during the 40s and 50s was a jazz lover's Mecca. Tea dances here were to music by Gösta Tönnes, who was in every way Harry Arnold's equal.

For dancing you would often go to Amiralen, and for a meal between turns on the dance floor you could go upstairs for one of the dozen or so standard items on the menu. Good food, but the best thing of all was the view across the dance floor. There was dancing at Amiralen on Wednesdays, Saturdays and Sundays.

For a grand tour of Malmö the main artery would be "the Critical Curve", along Södergatan and "The Riviera" between Engelbrektsgatan and Södergatan, where youngsters would stroll after school but above all in the evenings. Cinema time was between seven and nine, and after a successful café visit your evening would end at midnight, usually very quietly and decorously.

Outside Malmö, Falsterbohus was the star attraction. The cuisine was exquisite, and the music was provided by stars like Putte Wickman and Reynold Svensson. The Lecouna Cuban Boys were also a permanent feature in the 1960s, arriving in Falsterbohus for one summer season after another, to put the regulars in Latin American mood.

venska Dagbladet Snällposten N:r 119 Fredagen den 5 Maj

PALLADIUM
7,30 o. 9,15 Barnförbjuden!
Lew Ayres — Lynne Carver
Lionel Barrymore
UNGE dr KILDARE
En spännande film som skiljer sig från det gamla vanliga vi bruka få se om "män i vitt".
— Metro-Goldwyn-Mayer —
Bilj.-kont. öppnas kl. 4,30. T. 28800.

CAPITOL
7,15 o. 9,15 Barnförbjuden!
3:dje och sista succèsveckan!
Signe Hasso - Sture Lagerwall
VI TVÅ
Bilj.-kont. öppnas kl. 4,30. T. 1750

GÖTA
7,30 o. 9,15 Barntill
2:dra veckan!
POLTAVA
Rysk storfilm med grandi
bataljscener.
Bilj.-kont. öppnas kl. 4,30. Te

SCALA I ny tal- och lju
6. 7,30. 9,15. På västfronten
T. 26824. B. F. vår tids största

LANDSTINGS
I afton kl. 8
(Debut) KONS

SCANIA
Obs.! 7.15 o. 9.15. Barnförbjuden.
CLAUDETTE COLBERT o. HERBERT MARSHALL i
ZAZA
Den personifierade romantiken i glädjens, sorglöshetens och can-cans stad — Paris.
PARAMOUNT- och S. F.-REVY.
S. F.-reportage från 1 Maj — Statsministern talar i veckans S. F.-revy.
Förköp 12-3. Tel. 26387. Ord. pr. eft. 5. Tel. salong 26387, balkong 26386.

CRAB "Underbar!" SvD.
Den världsbekanta vildmarksfilmen
7.30, 9.15 Bt. SEQUOIA

Rio S. Förstadsg. 29
7.15 o. 9.15. Barnf. Förk. 12-3. Ord. pr. eft. 5. Tel. 75640.
Viviane ROMANCE
Pierre Renoir - Louis Jouvet i
MALTESARENS HUS
Raffinerad - Diskuterad - Applåderad

Grand Drottningtorget
7.15 o. 9.15. Barnt. Bilj. fr. 5. T. 28804.
:de veckan!

THURE LARS
ASTA NORGA
Efraim
Ryska Balettskola
Medverkande Solodansösen
Thaisia Trofimowitsch och

MUSHROOM BUTTONS AU GRATIN

with double-coated celeriac

Serves 4

INGREDIENTS:

1 large celeriac root
1 egg
1 dl white flour
1 dl dry breadcrumbs
salt, pepper
cooking fat for frying
12 large button mushrooms
200 g soft cheese, e.g. Vacherol

PROCEDURE:

1. Peel the celeriac with an ordinary knife. Cut it into slices about 1 cm thick and divide these in quarters.
2. Blanch them (i.e. boil lightly) in slightly salted water until they soften a little.
3. Get out three plates. Break the egg and mix it with 1 tbsp. water on one of the plates. Pour the flour onto another plate and the dried breadcrumbs, mixed with a little salt and pepper, on the third.
4. Now double-coat the bits of celeriac by dipping them first in the flour, then in the egg and lastly in the dried breadcumbs.
5. Fry in a frying pan in plenty of fat over a low flame for 3 or 5 minutes on each side or till nicely browned.
6. Remove the stems of the mushrooms. Chop the stems into small dice and put them inside the inverted tops.
7. Put a piece of cheese on each top and gratinate in the oven at 200°C until the cheese melts and bubbles.
8. Serve as a starter or appetiser.

COOKS COMMENT

Vegetarian dishes are perhaps not the first thing that comes to mind on the subject of Scanian food, but times have changed and the Scanian kitchen with them. And anyway, vegetable eating isn't exactly a new invention. You often need something quick and easy, so what about this for a trouble-free starter? The raw materials are easy to get hold of. The soft cheese may be a problem, but use another cheese if you have to.

TERRINE OF SALMON AND LEMON SOLE

with raspberry vinaigrette

Serves 4

INGREDIENTS:

1 side of fresh salmon, about 1–1 1/2 kg
800 g lemon sole fillets
salt, pepper
1 dl raspberries
3 tbsp. red wine vinegar
1 dl cold-pressed rape seed oil (or olive oil)

PROCEDURE:

For this recipe you need an oblong loaf tin or some other oven-proof container, about 5 cm deep and 25-30 cm long. You will also need a mixer or food processor and heat-resistant cling foil or grease-proof paper.

1. Extract all the pin bones from the fillet of salmon then slice it thinly like gravad lax.
2. Divide the double lemon sole fillets into single fillets.
3. Line the tin with the cling foil/ grease-proof paper. Place the slices of salmon in the tin so that they hang over the sides but cover the bottom. Salt them. Now add a layer of lemon sole fillet, salt them, then another layer of salmon and so on all the way to the top. Fold over your first slices of salmon - the ones hanging over the side - and fold over the cling foil/ grease-proof paper as well, to cover the tin.
4. Bake in the oven at 100°C for 30 minutes or until the terrine is done all the way through. Then leave it to cool in the fridge.
5. Now for the raspberry vinaigrette sauce. Run the raspberries in the mixer. Strain off the juice into a bowl, add the vinegar and oil, mix well and add salt and pepper to taste.
6. When the terrine is thoroughly chilled, cut it up into slices about 1 cm thick, using a really sharp knife.
7. Serve the slices on a bed of lettuce with the vinaigrette. Fresh raspberries make a good garnish.

COOKS COMMENT

Sometimes we call it pâté and lately it has become more modern to say terrine. Personally I go by whether you have minced the fish or used it whole, as I have here. By using fish of two different colours, you get a nicely patterned cross-section.

TERRINE OF GOOSE LIVER IN VEAL FARCE

enclosed in ham with a cress-flavoured orange salad

Serves 4–8

INGREDIENTS:

GOOSE LIVER TERRINE:
(or alternatively, a *pâté de foie gras* from the shop)
250 g butter
200 g goose liver
1 clove of garlic
2 dl Madeira, reduced to 1/2 dl
3 pinches of saltpetre
3 pinches of sugar
2 tsp. salt
white pepper (preferably milled)
4 leaves of gelatine
1/2 onion
200 g minced veal
salt, pepper
2 big oranges (or 4 small ones)
1 pot of cress
100–150 g sliced smoked ham

PROCEDURE:
For this recipe you need a mixer or food processor and an oven-proof oblong tin about 3 cm high and 25–30 cm long (a loaf tin, for example).
1. Make the goose liver terrine by first clarifying the butter (melt it, transfer to a bowl and pour off the sediment).
2. Mix the liver with the garlic and reduced Madeira.
3. Fold in the clarified butter, saltpetre, sugar, salt and a couple of twists from the pepper mill.
4. Put the gelatine leaves to soak in a bowl of water. Then wring them out and dissolve them in a saucepan over a gentle flame. Fold the gelatine into the liver mixture.
5. Pour the mixture into the oven-proof tin and bake in the oven at 90°C for about an hour. Leave the terrine to cool completely in the fridge (1 day).

If you get pâté de foie gras from the shop, start reading from here:
1. Chop the onion as fine as you can.
2. Mix the minced veal and onion, adding about 1 tsp. salt and 1/2 pinch of pepper, according to taste.
3. If the terrine is quite cold or has set in the fridge, turn it out. Now put the slices of ham in the tin, with their ends hanging over the side (so they can be folded over later).
4. Half-fill the tin with the veal farce mixture. Put the goose liver terrine in the middle and then top up with more veal farce so that the goose liver terrine is completely covered. Turn up the ends of the ham slices and cover the whole thing with heat-resistant cling foil or aluminium foil.
5. Bake in the oven at 100°C for about 40 minutes or until the farce is firm. Put in the fridge to cool completely.
6. Peel the oranges and cut out segments without going right through the outer edge – so as to get a "saw-tooth" pattern.
7. Transfer the orange segments to a plate – in a fan shape, for example – and then use the scissors to scatter cress on each place.
8. Now cut the (thoroughly chilled) veal and goose liver terrine into thin slices and put these on top of the orange salad.
Send it up!

COLD GLAZED BREAST OF PHEASANT

served on apple salad

Serves 4

INGREDIENTS:

4 filleted breasts of pheasant (or 2 pheasants)
salt, pepper
cooking fat for frying
3 differently coloured paprikas
truffle or polypore (*Scutiger ovinus*)
the green part of two leek leaves
1 orange
Jelly Aspic (available in well-stocked shops) or clear, reduced beef stock
2 tbsp. honey (runny preferred)
1/2 dl cooking oil
1/2 dl side of vinegar
4 apples (sweet and tasty)
a few leaves of lollo rosso lettuce
a few leaves of crisphead lettuce
a few leaves of ruccola lettuce

PROCEDURE:

1. Remove the pheasant breasts, unless you have bought them already filleted. Salt and pepper them, then fry them in a little fat, on both sides, for not more than 5 minutes over a relatively high flame.
2. Wrap the fillets in grease-proof paper and put them in a warming cabinet or in the oven at the lowest possible temperature. The "rest" will make them tender and juicy. Remove them about 30 minutes later, open the packet and put them to cool completely.
3. De-seed the paprikas and divide them in four. Remove the white pith as well.
4. Cut out small oval and round pieces of the paprika (and perhaps the black truffle or mushroom as well), so that you can make small flowers and other decorative patterns. The green of the leek, for example, can be cut into leaves for the "flowers". If you slice the oranges thinly, this gives you another chance of cutting out attractive decorations.
5. Place the decorations on the cold pheasant breasts.
6. Make the meat jelly by following the instructions on the packet, or else warm the "genuine" jelly in a pan on the hob until it runs. Cover the pheasant breasts with the jelly and put to cool in the fridge.
7. Mix a vinaigrette sauce of honey (heat it first if it isn't already running), oil and vinegar.
8. De-core the apples and slice them or cut them up. Rinse the lettuce. Make a bed of all the different kinds of lettuce, together with the pieces of apple, and pour on the vinaigrette.
9. If you feel like it, tidy up the breasts of pheasant by trimming the jelly neatly along the edges. Place them on your wonderful bed of lettuce and serve.

MUSHROOM-FILLED HEAD OF LETTUCE AU GRATIN

with herb-flavoured oil

Serves 4

INGREDIENTS:
4 lettuce heads
250 g button mushrooms
1/2 onion
a good, hard cheese
1 dl cooking oil
1 bundle of mixed fresh herbs
salt, pepper

PROCEDURE:
For this recipe you need a mixer or food processor.
1. Rinse the lettuce thoroughly, carefully cutting away the outermost, brown part of the stalk.
2. Divide each button mushroom in four and slice the onion thinly.
3. Place the heads of lettuce in a greased oven-proof dish and spread the mushroom pieces and onion slices over them.
4. Put a few slices of cheese on top of each lettuce head.
5. Bake quickly in the oven: 5 minutes at 150°.
6. Meantime, mix the oil and herbs, adding salt and pepper to taste.
7. Remove the lettuce, pour on the herb oil and serve.

SMOKED LAMB AND ROOT VEGETABLES IN ASPIC

on a fruit salad of cache, ruccola, crisphead and lollo rosso lettuce

Serves 4

INGREDIENTS:
1 head of lollo rosso
1 head of crisphead lettuce
1 box mache lettuce
1 box ruccola lettuce
400 g smoked lamb
2 same-sized carrots
2 parsnips
Jelly Aspic (available in well-stocked shops) meat jelly
1 pot of mint
1 dl cooking oil
1 tbsp. sugar
1 orange
1 apple
1 pear

PROCEDURE:
For this recipe you need an oblong mould or tin.
1. Rinse the lettuce thoroughly.
2. Dice the smoked lamb very small. Peel the root vegetables and boil them in lightly salted water until they are soft.
3. Put half the lamb in the mould, put the root vegetables on top of that and then add the rest of the lamb.
4. Make the jelly as instructed on the packet and then top up your mould with it. Put in the fridge to set.
5. Run the mint in a mixer or chop it fine and mix it with the oil and sugar.
6. Peel the orange. De-core the apple and pear and chop all fruit very small.
7. Cut or tear up the lollo rosso and crisphead lettuce and mix them with the other lettuce and the pieces of fruit.
8. Turn out the aspic and slice it with a really sharp, thin knife. (N.B. Take care to "saw" all the time. If you press too hard you will spoil the slices.) It helps if you warm the knife first.
9. Put the mixed salad on plates and serve with slices of the aspic. Pour the mint oil over the salad. A slice of fried coarse bread goes well with this one.

PLAICE FRIED IN BUTTER

on pieces of apple and onion braised in honey,
with a slow-melting lovage-flavoured green cheese

Serves 4

INGREDIENTS:
1 pot/bunch of lovage
1 red onion
1 ordinary onion
1/2 leek
1 l. cultured milk (*filmjölk* in Swedish)
100 g butter
salt, pepper
2 apples
4 large plaice
fat for frying (butter preferably)
1/2 dl honey

PROCEDURE:
1. Chop the lovage fine.
2. Peel the onion, trim and carefully rinse the leek.
3. Bring the cultured milk to the boil so that it granulates properly. Strain it through a coffee filter or a very fine sieve.
4. Blend the white mixture with the butter and the chopped herb. Add salt and pepper to taste and then transfer to the fridge.
5. De-core the apples, then chop them and the onions very small.
6. Fry the fish whole in a frying pan with a knob of butter. Keep it warm.
7. Toss the pieces of apple and onion in a frying pan with a little fat. Pour on the honey and reduce slightly.
8. Put out this mixture on four plates, put the warm fish on that and top with a little green cheese to melt and run over the whole thing.

COOK'S COMMENT

The inspiration here comes from what we may call a Danish/Swedish classic: batter-fried Fredrikshamn plaice with remoulade sauce. A modern variant, using green cheese, apple, honey, onion and lovage, is our way of updating it and making it a little bit leaner. But I draw the line at the butter. That gives the whole thing character, so it shouldn't be left out.

Culinary links

Denmark and Sweden have had a great deal in common where eating habits are concerned. And small wonder, with Öresund joining both people and raw materials together.

Herring is one of those raw materials. It used to be dried or salted down, today it is pickled in all sorts of ways on both sides of the narrow divide. On the Swedish side you have, for example, Spången's sherry herring, Margaretetorp's Möllare herring and the apple and caraway herring of Häckeberga Wärdshus. If your journey takes you past Hansens Familiehave at Zoo in Copenhagen you could do worse than go for their *porresild*, a delicious concoction involving leek and garlic.

If you would like to see what things were like, more or less, a hundred years or so ago, travel to Anholt. There they still eat their spiced herring the original way, with potatoes stewed in milk. This "Bornholm herring" is probably the link between Denmark and Sweden.

Now fish wasn't the whole story in this part of the world. There was porridge too, for example. Usually this meant water porridge or meal porridge. If you lived in Fyen you might get buckwheat porridge, and if you were well off it would sometimes be rice porridge. To the rest of the world nowadays, this porridge tradition looks exotically Nordic.

As regards meat, Denmark and Southern Sweden share a common

across the water

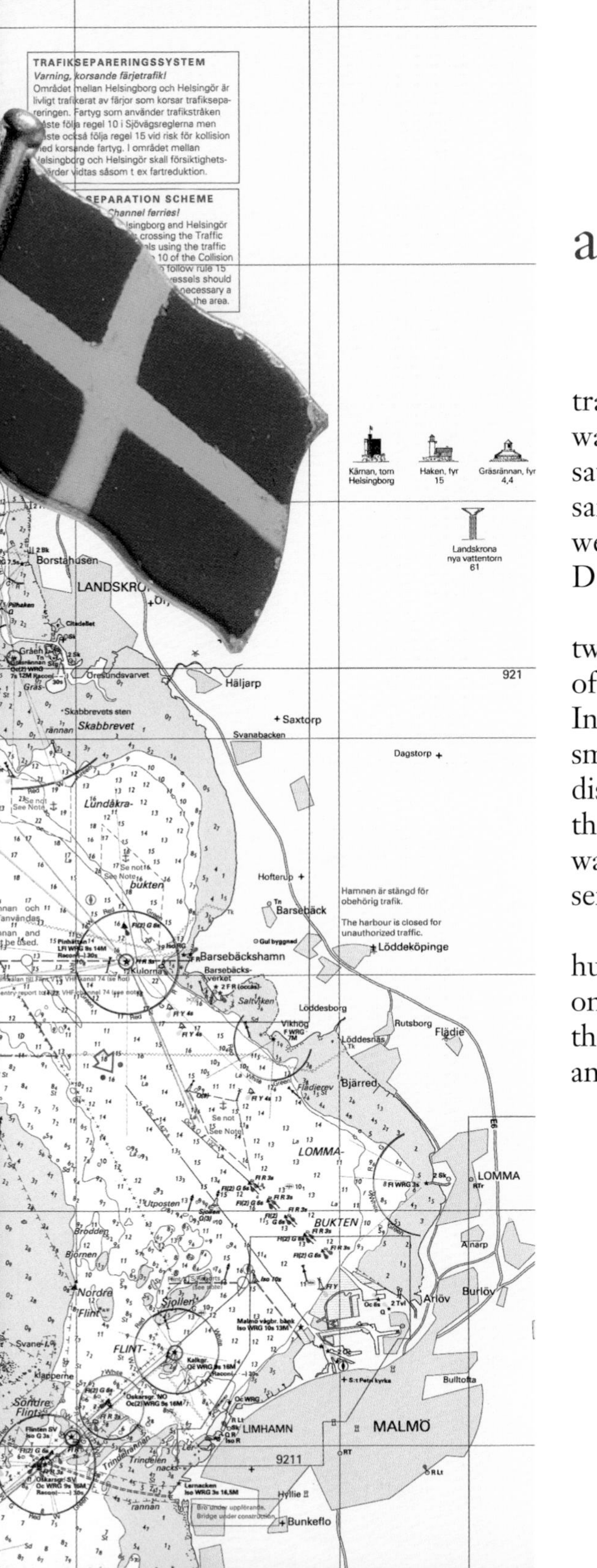

tradition of pork and goose. Pigmeat was (and still is) turned into brawn, sausage and steak. We both have the same way of roasting our goose, but we have ours in November and the Danes have theirs at Christmas.

When talking of similarities between Skåne and Denmark, we must of course remember the smorgasbord. Indeed one should never forget it. The smorgasbord started off as a generous display and presentation of the best the house could offer. Sometimes it was a Jacob's joint, with each guest sending on a contribution in advance.

There are any number of dishes for hungry tummies which are the same on both sides of Öresund. One of them is *brännesnuda*, a mixture of gruel and soup, boiled with de-salted pigmeat and barley groats. Perhaps not the commonest dishes, but they still make it. Then there is the more familiar *pytt-i-panna*, known in Denmark as *biksemad*. They differ in name but they taste the same and they look pretty well the same too. On the other hand there is a world of difference between Swedish *äppelkaka* and Denmark's *æblekage*, because the Swedish version has pieces of apple baked into it.

So much for the food, but one could go on indefinitely about drink. Beer and schnapps exist on both sides of the water, and generally speaking the Scanians are more disposed to drink Danish than the other way round. But this, probably, is more a matter of preference and old prejudice than more fundamental cleavages.

Eating on board the Copenhagen ferries

Understandably, the cuisine on board the Copenhagen ferries was fairly limited, but it was no less appreciated for that. The first train ferry to ply between Malmö and Copenhagen was Danish and was called *Kronprinsessan Louise*. She was taken into service in 1892, and eight years later was joined by the classic *Malmö*. Then came the long succession of "big boats".

Travelling was easy enough, but eating could be more of a problem. Conditions, at any rate, were far from ideal. Right down to the days of the Köpenhamn, the galley was relegated to the bowels of the ship, only emerging on the main deck in the 1960s, on

board the Gripen. She was built in Århus and was a modern ship in more ways than one.

Innumerable Swedes and Danes have eaten their way across Öresund, revelling in the creations of legendary chef de cuisine Tage Stålbrand. The *Gripen* had six departures daily, starting from Malmö at 9.30. On the first crossing, eggs and bacon were served in the dining room, while in the cafeteria, which the Gripen was the first to provide on this route, they had to make do with sandwiches. There was a small first-class saloon at the very top, with table service, but all you could get was coffee, tea or beer - a high-class café, in other words.

Then came lunchtime. In the dining room they served three kinds of cut sandwiches and a number of warm dishes. The latter alternated between fish fried in batter with remoulade sauce, "English beef" and Wiener schnitzel. Sometimes there would be boiled veal with dill sauce and roast pork with the crispest of crackling. There was a short à la carte menu, but that was hidden away and only got out when expressly asked for by seasoned travellers who knew of its existence. The last two departures of the day were always fully subscribed, ensuring a festive mood in the dining room.

The *Gripen* dining room could seat up to 150 guests, ministered to by a head waiter and his seven underlings. Behind the scenes there were three cooks, seven cold buffet ladies and a number of washers-up.

If you wanted more than just food, you could cross over by Centrumlinjen, which had dancing on board. If you also wanted more to drink and the 2.5 cl of spirits per passenger and trip dictated by government, that could also be arranged, because the ration was worked out at an average for the full day, so there was plenty to be had if you were up to it.

You could also have a conference on board. Both the *Gripen* and the

Cheerful group of cold buffet ladies and cooks on one of all the indefatigable Copenhagen ferries, photographed outside the galley sometime in 1949 or 1950.

Öresund were converted to look after groups wanting to sit together - just talking business, of course.

Gradually the menu changed, under the influence of growing competition both from restaurants on shore and between the boats themselves. One or two things never changed, though. The herring plate was indispensable, and the Danes always made their own sandwiches, their only contribution to profits being through what they drank in the dining room.

Now they can eat their sandwiches on the train crossing the bridge.

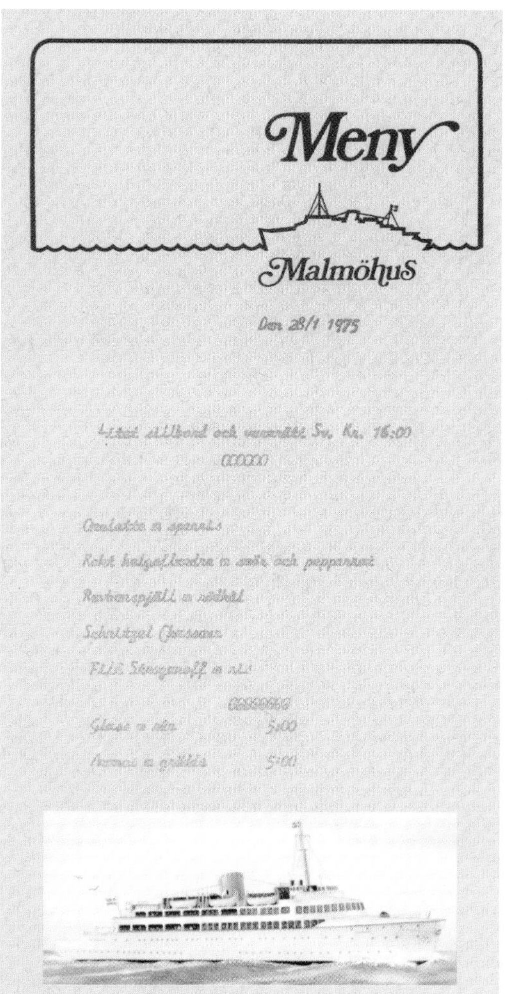

Meny

Malmöhus

Den 28/1 1975

Litet sillbord och varmrätt Sv. Kr. 16:00

Omelette m spenat

Rökt helgeflundra m smör och pepparrot

Revbensspjäll m rödkål

Schnitzel Chasseur

Filé Stroganoff m ris

Glass m [illegible] 5:00

Ananas m grädde 5:00

FILLET OF SALMON COATED WITH HAZELNUTS AND BREADCRUMBS

with fennel-flavoured fermented cream and raw-fried potato en cocotte

Serves 4

INGREDIENTS:
1 kg potatoes
1/2 leek
1/2 fennel head
1 bunch of parsley (preferably flat-leafed)
2 dl double cream
1 dl hazelnuts
800 g fillet of salmon
1/2 dl white flour
1 egg
cooking fat for frying (oil if possible)
salt, pepper
5 dl crème fraîche
1/2 dl fish stock
4 cl Pernod

PROCEDURE:
For this recipe you need four heat-resistant ramekins and a mixer.
1. Peel the potatoes and cut them into matchsticks. Rinse the leek and chop fine. Chop the fennel fine.
2. Mix the parsley with a few table-spoons of water, to give a green liquid.
3. Flavour the cream with the parsley liquid.
4. Chop the hazelnuts fine.
5. Divide the fillet of fish into four equal pieces, removing the skin.
6. Pour the flour onto one plate, beat the egg a little in another and pour the chopped hazelnuts onto a third.
7. Turn the fillets in the flour, then in the egg and lastly in the chopped nuts. Transfer to an oven-proof dish.
8. Raw-fry the potatoes in a frying pan with cooking fat, at maximum heat. When the potatoes seem ready, add the pieces of leek. Salt and pepper.
9. Fill the ramekins with the potato, pour on the flavoured cream and put the ramekins in the oven at 150°C for 10 or 15 minutes or until the cream is boiling nicely. Put the fish in the oven at the same time.
10. Pour a little fat into a saucepan and frizzle the fine-chopped fennel.
11. Pour on the crème fraîche, the fish stock and Pernod and bring to the boil, stirring all the time. Transfer to a mixer, give it a moderate blast and then return to the saucepan and bring to the boil again.
12. Serve the salmon with turned-out gratinated potatoes and the liquorice-tasting sauce.

POACHED ROULADE OF HALLIBUT AND TUNA

with lemon foam

Serves 4

INGREDIENTS:
1/2 onion
1 lemon
cooking fat
3 dl double cream
1/2 dl fish stock
1/2 dl white wine
salt, pepper
500 g fillet of tuna

PROCEDURE:
1. Peel the onion and chop fine. Juice the lemon.
2. Melt the onion in a saucepan with a little cooking fat. Pour on the cream, stock, wine and lemon juice and reduce. Add salt and pepper to taste. Put the sauce to one side for the time being.
3. Use a salad knife to cut both fillets into thin slices.
4. Take two slices, one of each sort, roll them together and secure with heat-resistant plastic or a toothpick.
5. Transfer the fish to a greased, oven-proof dish. Poach in the oven at 100°C for about 10 minutes. Turn off the oven and leave the fish where it is for a while.
6. To serve, bring the sauce to the boil, perhaps "spinning" it with a stick blender. Serve it on the same plate as the fish.

GRILLED FILLET OF COD ON A BED OF ONION AND CABBAGE

with a bacon and red wine sauce, served with herb-flavoured potato pancakes

Serves 4

INGREDIENTS:

1 kg floury potatoes
800 g fillet of cod (preferably with the scales removed but not the skin)
2–3 tbsp. cooking oil
1 leek
1/2 head red cabbage
1/2 head of savoy cabbage
2 onions
50 g bacon
1/2 dl veal stock
4 dl red wine
salt, pepper
thickening (arrowroot, cornflour or potato flour mixed with cold water)
1 bunch of chives
1 bunch of dill
1 bunch of parsley
about 100 g butter for mashing the potatoes and for frying
1 l. milk
4 eggs

PROCEDURE:

1. Peel the potatoes and boil them in lightly salted water.
2. Divide the fish into four large or several small pieces, put these on kitchen tissue and press them gently so that the tissue soaks up all the extra water. Now roll the pieces in cooking oil on a plate.
3. Split the leek down the middle and rinse it thoroughly under running cold water.

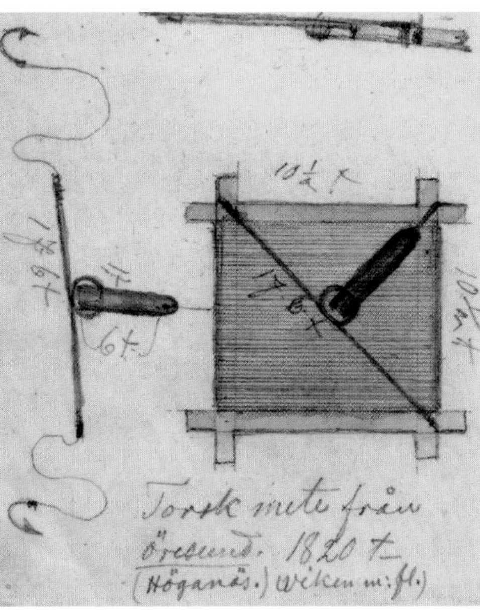

Cod fishing line from Öresund. Watercolour by Nils Månsson Mandelgren.

4. Tear, slice or otherwise divide the leek, the red cabbage, the savoy and 1 1/2 onions. Put to one side.
5. Chop the rest of the onion fine and cut up the bacon in small pieces.
6. Frizzle the bacon in a casserole, pour on 1/2 dl veal stock and the red wine and reduce for 10 minutes. Now add water to give the right strength, followed by salt and pepper to taste. Bring the sauce to the boil again and thicken to a suitable consistency. Put the sauce to one side.
7. Chop the chives, dill and parsley.
8. Mash the boiled potatoes with a pounder or a stick blender, after adding a knob of butter. Then pour on the milk and eggs and stir until smooth. Pour in the fine-chopped chives, dill and parsley and add salt and pepper to taste.
9. Put a knob of butter in the frying pan, make small pancakes of the potato mixture and brown on both sides. (For real neatness, you can put a crumpet ring or suchlike in the frying pan and pour the mixture into that.) Keep the pancakes warm.
10. Now you have to grill the pieces of fish, either outdoors or in a grill pan. (By giving each piece a quarter-

turn after grilling it for a while, you will produce the classic grill pattern we usually like to see.)

11. Frizzle the cabbage, leek and onion in a little fat.

12. Put the cabbage mixture on plates or a serving dish. Put the fish on top of that, pour the sauce all around and serve with the pancakes.

MUSHROOM SOUP

with pieces of game

Serves 4

INGREDIENTS:

1 onion
200–300 g fresh mushrooms (whatever you can get)
100 g game (preferably smoked venison or suchlike)
cooking fat for frying
1/2 dl balsamic vinegar
1 dl Madeira
100 g butter
salt, pepper

PROCEDURE:

1. Peel the onion and chop fine. Trim the mushrooms. Cut up the meat into 2 cm 2 pieces.
2. Frizzle the chopped onion with a quarter of the mushrooms in frying fat in a saucepan (for 2 or 3 minutes or until the onion and mushroom change colour a little). Pour on the vinegar and Madeira and reduce by about half.
3. Use a mixer or blender to make a smooth soup of this mixture and the butter. Transfer to a pan or bowl.
4. Frizzle the rest of the mushrooms in a little cooking fat in the saucepan. Add the meat and cook until brown.
5. Pour on the soup and bring to the boil. Add water, salt and pepper to taste. Serve immediately.

MINCED ELK VENISON BAKED AU GRATIN WITH GOAT'S MILK CHEESE

with beans and parsnips

Serves 4

INGREDIENTS:

300 g minced venison of elk
100 g minced pork
100 g goat's milk cheese (or more if you like)
2–3 parsnips
8-10 potatoes
1/2 onion
250 g beans (string beans, wax beans or others)
3 eggs
1 dl milk
cooking fat for frying
1 pinch of rosemary
1 pinch of thyme
1–2 juniper berries
salt, pepper

PROCEDURE:

1. Peel the parsnips and potatoes and cut them in thin round slices, chop the onion fine and half the beans.
2. Blanch (lightly boil) the potatoes in lightly salted water.
3. Break the eggs into a bowl and mix well with the milk. Add salt and pepper to taste.
4. Frizzle the parsnips and onion in a little fat on a medium to high flame, in a large casserole with a pinch of rosemary, a pinch of thyme and 1–2 crushed juniper berries.
5. Mix in the beans, followed by the minced venison and the minced pork. Stir all the time to make sure everything is thoroughly blended and the meat properly browned.
6. Last of all, add the potato and transfer the whole thing to an ovenproof dish. Slice the goat's cheese and lay or crumble it over the mixture.
7. Bake at the top of the oven at 225°C for about 10 minutes or until the cheese has changed colour a little.
8. Serve straight from the dish with a little crisp iceberg lettuce.

COOK'S COMMENT

Although the elk is not the commonest of big game animals in Skåne, migration has made it more common than it used to be, to our hunters' delight. I rather fancy the idea of including the elk in this book as a fully paid-up Scanian.

TOURNEDOS OF VENISON WRAPPED IN ROOT VEGETABLES

with a colourful mixture of potatoes and root vegetables and a parsnip sauce

Serves 4

INGREDIENTS:
250 g pale potatoes
250 g "Blue Congo" potatoes
6 large carrots
10 large parsnips
1 leek
1/2 dl white wine
3 dl double cream
salt, pepper
800 g fillet or saddle of venison
cooking fat for frying

PROCEDURE:
For this recipe you need a mixer or food processor.
1. Peel the potatoes and the root vegetables. Rinse the green part of the leek and cut into four long strips, one or two cm wide.
2. Blanch (cook until soft) 2 carrots, 2 parsnips and the strips of leek.
3. Now slice the four root vegetables lengthwise into slices about 2 mm thick (using a cheese slice, for example).
4. Divide two parsnips into smaller pieces and boil them in the wine and 5 dl water for 10 or 15 minutes or until they are really soft. Top up with water if necessary, so that nothing boils dry.
5. Pour off a little of the water and run the rest in your mixer or food processor. Return the mixture, which should now be quite thick, to the saucepan and dilute with the cream. Bring to the boil, add salt and pepper to taste.
6. Divide the rest of the root vegetables and potatoes to the preferred size and boil until soft in lightly salted water.
7. Divide the meat into four pieces. Fry them in a little fat in a frying pan for 1 or 2 minutes per side.
8. Wind the slices of carrot and parsnip round the meat and tie everything in place with the strips of leek.
9. Finish off with 5 or 7 minutes in the oven at about 100°C.
10. Serve the root vegetables and potato as a mixed salad together with the parsnip sauce and the packaged tournedos of venison.

COOK'S COMMENT

Keeping the root vegetables round the meat with just toothpicks isn't easy. It will simplify matters if you can get hold of "crepinette" (available from well-stocked butchers) to wind round. Eating a piece of meat as large as tournedos is perhaps not my personal favourite, but if it has to be done this could be the solution.

FILLET OF HARE ON A BED OF RASPBERRIES AND CELERY

with a chocolate-flavoured raspberry sauce and baked potato au gratin

Serves 4

INGREDIENTS:
8–10 fillets of hare
2 potatoes for baking
1/2 kg floury potatoes (King Edward, for example)
1 stick of celery
1/2 onion
50 g butter
1 egg
salt, pepper
cooking fat for frying
1/2 dl red wine
1/2 dl game stock
2 dl raspberries
100 g bitter dark cooking chocolate

PROCEDURE:
1. Remove all sinews from the meat. Rinse the potatoes and green vegetables thoroughly.
2. Bake the two big potatoes in the oven at 175°C for 15 minutes or until they seem ready.
3. Peel and boil the "ordinary" potatoes.
4. When these are soft enough, mash them to a purée together with the butter and egg. Add salt and pepper to taste.
5. Cut the celery in small cubes.
6. Chop the half-onion fine and "melt" the proceeds in a little fat in a saucepan. Pour on the wine and stock and reduce a little.
7. Add about 2 dl water and bring to the boil again. Now add 1/2 dl raspberries and the chocolate and make sure the latter melts completely. Add salt and pepper to taste.
8. Divide the baked potatoes. Use a forcing bag or a spoon to transfer the potato purée to the potato halves, giving each one a little pyramid. Bake in the oven at 200-225°C until they are a nice golden colour.
9. Fry the fillets of hare in a knob of cooking fat in the frying pan until they are nicely browned all over. Remove the meat, wrap it in greaseproof paper and aluminium foil and put it back in the pan to finish cooking in the remaining heat for about ten minutes.
10. Meanwhile frizzle the bits of celery in a little cooking fat in the frying pan. When they begin to change colour, pour on the rest of the raspberries and then remove everything from the pan immediately.
11. Put the frizzled mixture of celery and raspberries in the middle of a plate and pour the sauce round it. Slice or divide the fillets and put them on top of the mixture. Serve with the baked potato au gratin.

CHICKEN SCHNITZEL WITH FRUIT BRUNOISE FILLING

served with a chicken and prune sausage and a sweetish cider sauce

Serves 4

INGREDIENTS:

Sausage casings
2 whole chickens
1 carrot
1 parsnip
1/2 celeriac
1/2 onion
3–5 bay leaves
5 corns of white pepper
1 tsp. dried thyme
10 stoneless prunes
salt, pepper
2 apples
2 pears
5 dl apple cider
arrowroot or cornflour for thickening

PROCEDURE:

For this recipe you need a food processor with sausage-stuffing accessories for the meat grinder.

1. Put the salted casings in a bowl of cold water, to release the salt.
2. Cut out the fillets from the chicken and remove all other meat from the carcass.
3. Peel the root vegetables and onion and cut them in small pieces.
4. Make stock with the remainder of the carcass. Put it in a large saucepan together with the root vegetables, onion, bay leaves, white pepper and thyme. Cover generously with water.
5. Bring to the boil, skim and then simmer gently for an hour or so. Make sure it doesn't boil dry. While all this is happening, you can sort out the other details.
6. Chop the prunes into small pieces.
7. Run all the meat, except the fillets, through the meat grinder. Mix the jerky (mince) with salt and 2 or 3 turns of the (white) pepper mill, plus 2/3 of the prune fragments.
8. Remove the knives from your meat grinder and assemble the sausage funnel. Brush it with a little oil and pull on the casings.
9. Feed in the minced meat and tie your sausages at preferred intervals.
10. Boil the sausages gently for 15 minutes.
11. Rinse all the fruit and cut up small for a fruit salad, adding to it what is left of the prunes.
12. Make an incision down the length of each chicken fillet, taking care not to cut all the way through. Open the slits and fill them with the fruit salad. Roll them up, and then roll them in heat-resistant cling foil, or else pin them together with a toothpick each.
13. Roast your schnitzels in the oven at 100°C for 30 minutes.
14. Strain the stock in a new saucepan and pour on the cider. Boil for another 10 minutes.
15. Add salt and pepper to taste, and perhaps too a tiny bit of sugar because the sauce needs to be a little sweet and salt. Thicken with cornflour or arrowroot mixed with cold water.
16. Remove the cling foil from the schnitzels and fry them in a little fat, to give them a nice golden colour.
17. Serve the schnitzels, sausage and sauce, preferably with a few wedges of fried potato.

COOK'S COMMENT

The word schnitzel is most often associated with a double-coated piece of meat. This old fashioned, high-fat method isn't really what the name means. A schnitzel, by definition, is a thin slice of meat, fish, poultry or vegetable. A little filling of fine-chopped fruit, a sweet-and-sour sauce and a prune-flavoured sausage bring the whole thing, in my opinion, successfully up to date.

EGG DESSERT OF DEWBERRY OR BLACKBERRY

served with vanilla crème fraîche

Serves 4–6

INGREDIENTS:
1 1/2 dl white flour
5 egg yolks
1 vanilla pod
2 1/2 dl milk
2 tbsp. butter
1 l. dewberries/blackberries
1/2 dl sugar
1/2 tsp. salt
fat for greasing the dish
(optional: 3 dl crème fraîche flavoured to taste with vanilla sugar)

PROCEDURE:
1. Melt the butter in a saucepan and stir in the flour. Now stir in the milk and bring to the boil, stirring continuously.
2. Stir in the egg yolks. Split the vanilla pod down the middle and scrape the seeds into the mixture. Stir in salt and sugar as well. Put to one side.
3. Grease an oven-proof pie dish (about 30 cm in diameter and with a rim about 5 cm high).
4. Spread out the berries in the dish and pour on the mixture.
5. Gratinate in the oven at 175°C for about 30 minutes or until it has turned a nice golden brown.
6. Serve straight from the dish. For a really fresh accompaniment, mix crème fraîche with a little vanilla sugar.

COOK'S COMMENT

Not exactly a pie. Berries and sauce in one, you might say. Rather like a French clafoutis.

WINTER

Grizzly winter

Grizzly winter
snowed straight down at first
but quiet as a Christmas card
then horizontally
now everything's in chaos.
Skåne winters are worse
than the sheep's nightmares
What do the sheep dream?
They have banked everything
on one scenario:
being in clover!

CARL MAGNUS VON SETH
From "Får – ännu är gräset grönt", 1981

Winter food

Festival food apart, the diet was a balancing act between fresh food and preserves. At the beginning of the season there was still a good deal of fresh food left over from slaughter and harvest, but there were grimmer times ahead, and so the winter table soon had to be adapted to the store that had been put by in salt troughs, corn bins and larders.

Salt herring featured in various guises (including even soup), so did salt pork, and every now and then there would be a dried breast of goose, a smoked leg of mutton, but they were special treats.

Then there was buckwheat porridge, oatmeal porridge and barley porridge, as well as bread, which was often a *kavring* baked on both sides. Turnips, cabbage and, eventually during the 19th century, potato completed the picture. Home-brewed malt beer was the usual drink.

But in many places, as we have already seen, it was very short commons, especially for the servants. When the farm lads found their diet getting too meagre or monotonous, they could come out with couplets like this one, in time to the dinner bell:

Sour herring and blue gruel,
Sour herring and blue gruel.

There are any number of verses like this to show how disgruntled the servants could get over their masters' meanness. Here is another one:

One day a week, we are given meat
From the starveling ox that dropped dead in the street,
But herring is the thing they give us every day
And a jug or two of butter milk all mixed with curds and whey.

Before the coming of the iron stove, most food was cooked over the open fire or on the embers in the combined kitchen range and fireplace to be seen in old Scanian farmhouses. The cooking pot would often contain a mixture of meat or fish, turnips and other roots, plus water. This soup or broth would be put into a big bowl which was set in the middle of the table. Everyone would eat from this bowl, each with his or her own spoon.

Arrival of the herring. Today herring fishing started in earnest at Kullen. Five boats have trawled off Mölle and caught 20 or 25 valar each. The price is 2:25 or 3 crowns per val.

Ola Persson of Perstorp butchering the Christmas pig.
Photo taken by his son, Per Stjernberg, in about 1900.

In pre-industrial Scanian society, Christmas often began with dipping in the pot at midday.

"Dinner would be about midday. A big pot of pork was put on the boil. The stock was left in the pot, or else it was poured into a big dish and several slices of bread dipped into it," a note from Herrestad tells us. "As well as the dish, the schnapps jar was put out both first and last."

Note that what they boiled in those days was not ham as we know it today but big lumps of pork. The lean ham we buy today doesn't represent a very old tradition, though we like to think it does. One Christmas Eve speciality with a very ancient history, on the other hand, is *lutfisk*, which in Skåne was often accompanied by mustard sauce and green peas. In pre-Reformation times (before the 1520s), Christmas was preceded by a 40-day fast, which meant that meat wasn't allowed till the morning of Christmas day. Fish was, on the other hand, which explains why we eat *lutfisk* on Christmas Eve. Just for the record, veal, which was ever so com-

After the meal the spoons would be wiped on trouser legs and put away in the spoon drawer of the table until next time.

In an autobiography describing life in Österlen at about the turn of the century, Selma Frode Kristensson writes: "Everyone ate from the same dish. We used horn spoons. Everyone had their own. The women used to wipe theirs on their aprons when the meal was over, the men would wipe theirs on the backs of their trousers."

Every now and again, though, the dark season of the year was lit up by festivals and celebrations, and food and drink were expected to flow accordingly. Once again, housewives were put to the test.

"The old song tells us that Christmas lasts until Easter but a Scanian housewife could have said that it started on St Michael's, at the end of October. At any rate, from then on, all her time was spent making the preparations at home which had to be completed by Christmas Eve and the results of which, both for that evening and for the festivals that followed, was a kind of cachet or judgement of her domestic competence." Thus Nanna Lundh-Eriksson, in her classic *Skånsk mat och skånska seder*, published in 1934.

May you dip into the pot like this happy little tot,
and may Yuletide joy and grace be upon you and your place.

mon on the east coast, sometimes replaced cod or saithe on Christmas Eve in eastern Skåne. Before the evening meal, the custom was to make "Christmas heaps" for the servants and the youngest children. In north-eastern Skåne, for example: "Every person – child, servant girl and farmhand – had to have their Christmas heap, put out in their place at the table on Christmas Eve. The Christmas heap was a small cake of rye bread, two pretzels of barley flour, a handful of nuts, a handful of dried fruit, two fresh apples and a pair of stockings for the farmhand or, for the servant girl, cloth for making an apron. She had to make it up herself - you couldn't buy ready-made ones in those days.

"Then Mother lit the candles and the real Christmas Eve began. Father sat at the end of the table and next to him a seat was reserved for Mother. The rest of us sat in order of age and authority. When the food had been brought in, Mother and the other women would all sit down at the table."

What was on the table, then, for this, the most important festive evening of the whole year? In present-day terms it is best described as a smörgåsbord of epic proportions. Just as with other festivals, the meat and drink (both on Christmas Eve and at subsequent festivities) mirrored the farm's economic and social status, which made it very important to keep up appearances.

A Christmas table description from central Skåne begins: "The food consisted of bread, sweet-sour and sifted rye, pigs' trotters and beetroot. After that we had fish." The list continues with spare ribs, mock brawn, collared brawn, black pudding, pork sausage, boiled sausage and cabbage (both kale and fried cabbage). Roast goose or duck was also part of the old Scanian Christmas table, not forgetting all the different kinds of pork. Then there was the Christmas cheer - home-brewed beer and spiced schnapps. Even if not all these things were to be seen on the same Christmas table, every household pulled out all the available stops.

And then there was porridge. Skåne was a prime granary, and so porridge was everyday food. On high days and holidays, the ordinary rye flour was replaced with barley groats or buckwheat, made if possible with milk instead of water. Milk being in short supply, especially during wintertime (when the cows were on starvation diet and often dried up completely), sometimes the porridge was made with malt liquor. "Porridge" made with rice - an expensive imported commodity - didn't catch on until the closing years of the 19th century.

Custom required you to "rhyme to the porridge", at all events if you were lucky or unlucky enough to scoop up the almond. These occasional rhymes were a fine opportunity for cocking a snook at a niggardly master or setting your cap at a man or woman you fancied. For example:

Porridge made our festival,
Pity the master ate it all.

If I rhyme for the porridge, then let it be said
That the girl I love will take me to bed.

The meal ended with a prayer of thanks, then people got up from the table for games of different kinds - pulling the ox, taming the steer, bumming the pitchfork, odds and evens and various other high jinks.

Christmas food, then, is traditional but changeable. Ancient dishes mingle with new creations, and that's the way it has always been. The changes often pass unnoticed, but they happen. And this is a strength, not a weakness. No tradition can survive without an inherent capacity for change. This applies to gastronomy and to other kinds of culture. One need only mention the case of two newly-weds organising their own Christmas apart from their parents, or the immigrant family trying to marry their Christmas to Sweden's.

Anne and Lucia

Christmas never came unprepared. Advent was very important in the society of yesterday, with the feasts of St Anne and Lucia as important staging posts.

The First Sunday in Advent marked the beginning of the Church's year and of many preparations for Christmas. Originally it also ushered in the pre-Christmas fast, a meatless period until the morning of Christmas day. Though strict observance is a thing of the remote past, for a long time it was felt that the approach of Christmas demanded special tranquillity. There were preparations to be made, of course, but the everyday activities of weaving, spinning and overhauling farm implements were left to one side.

Tranquillity or no tranquillity, then as now, of course, Advent was a period of rising expectation, but the Swedish customs of Advent candles and Christmas calendars are fairly recent innovations. The Advent candles were introduced by Archbishop Nathan Söderblom in about 1900, while the Advent calendar, a German idea, started to catch on in the 1930s. The Advent star too is of German origin. The first one in Sweden is said to have been lit in Lund in 1912 by the German-born wife of a professor.

By *St Anne's Day*, 9th December, the Christmas brew must be sufficiently fermented for the neighbours to be treated to a jar of young beer. It was equally common, though, for the feast of St Thomas, 21st December, to be taken as the red-letter day for brewing. Presumably this was a better idea, beer in those days being a short-lived, perishable product. Besides, if it were brewed too early, perhaps there would be none left when Christmas finally came. Another task for St Anne's Day was steeping the *lutfisk* (stockfish).

Lucia, 13th December. Lucia celebrations as we know them today are a very Swedish custom with practically no counterpart in any other country except for Swedish Finland and, in more recent years, Denmark and Norway. We do not know exactly how the custom arose. The story begins with the Sicilian legend of a

Lucia, photographed in Malmö in 1933 by Bebbe Ohm.

young girl being stoned to death on account of her faith and goodness. From then the legend spread northwards through Europe, and in Sweden, for some unknown reason, it gained a special foothold in Värmland and Västergötland. 13th December also marked the winter solstice in the old calendar (in force until 1753), which perhaps explains why this generous young lady should be dressed in white and adorned with candles, as a counterpoise to the maximum winter darkness.

Lucia celebrations did not become a really universal, official custom until 1929, when the newspaper *Stockholms Dagblad* organised a Lucia procession through the streets of Stockholm. That event introduced the competitive element, with the nomination of the annual Lucia from a pictorial voting list for the newspaper's readers to choose from.

The curly shape of the "Lucia cat" betrays its affinity to the shewbread of earlier times – that is, bread so cunningly crafted that it was only meant to be looked at. Saffron - an expensive luxury - was added to enhance the status of the bread and the occasion.

Father Christmas and his presents

Many children today envisage Father Christmas (*Tomten*) as a plump, jovial old man with a white beard and a resounding "ho, ho, ho" laugh. He comes flying through the air on his reindeer sled on Christmas night, lands on the house tops, climbs down the chimneys and puts presents in the stockings which children have hung up for the purpose. Perhaps instead of the Swedish *tomte* he now goes by the Disney-speak appellation of Santa.

The good old Swedish Father Christmas isn't really as old as he looks. He began to evolve just over a hundred years ago, when his pedigree showed two lines of descent: one going back to ancient Christian tradition, the other to native heathendom.

During the 4th century the city of Myrra, in what is now Turkey, had a Bishop called Nicholas. The Roman Emperor of the day found Christianity irksome, with the result that Nicholas got thrown into prison every now and again. He had a reputation for generosity, especially where children were concerned. This eventually gave rise to the image of St Nicholas as the kind old man with the beard, doling out presents to the children. Variously named, he has lived on in Europe down to the present day, and Dutch settlers brought him to the USA in the 17th century. There he came to be known as Santa Claus or, nowadays, just plain Santa.

The old Swedish brownie was, by tradition, quite different from St Nicholas. The brownie (also *Tomten*) was a little grey figure, tremendously strong but evil-tempered. He lived somewhere in the out buildings, and if you kept well in with him he would bring happiness and prosperity to the farm.

"But," someone from Luggude tells us, "if he didn't get his porridge of an evening, or if you made fun of him or were nasty to him, he would get angry and before long would take away from the house more than he had obtained for it previously, making it poor instead of rich."

Our present-day brownie was extricated from the tangle of folklore precedent by the artist Jenny Nyström. She already began drawing and painting brownies in the 1870s, and

in due course she was to paint tens of thousands of brownie scenes for Christmas cards, Christmas tree decorations, wrapping paper and book illustrations.

To the children, Santa's presents are the main ingredient of Christmas, and this is made only too clear by the onset of Yuletide commerce, several weeks before the event. Things weren't quite like that in the old days, but the custom of Christmas giving is a very ancient one. From Väsby in the 1860s we are told: "After a Christmas box had been thrown in, the nimblest of the men were eager to catch up with the giver before it was too late, and bring him into the cottage. They were seldom able to catch the fugitive, however, and so they had to guess who it was, and often this could be deduced from the nature of the gift." This story also explains the etymology of the Swedish for Christmas present, *julklapp* – literally: "Christmas knock". In other words, something you quickly throw in through the door after first knocking and opening.

Christmas night and early morning service

The night between Christmas Eve and Christmas Day was redolent of mystery. Powerful forces were believed to be in motion, on the strength of both Christian and pre-Christian beliefs. People had to protect themselves as best they could against the evil ones. A metal cross – two knives laid crosswise on the threshold of the outer door, for example – was one way, the idea being that the powers of evil would then be kept at bay.

The gravity of this night made it especially suitable for augury and fortune-telling, especially with the aid of candles. For example, you can sit round a lighted candle and look to see in whose direction the wick bent first. Woe betide them, because they would be the first to die. Presumably it was mostly young people who indulged, a little playfully, in this kind of necromancy.

Another way of looking into the future was by "going the annual round". This is how it was done. On Christmas Eve you had to abstain completely from food and drink, and you must not speak to anyone. That evening you went to the churchyard and groped your way backwards three times round the church, still maintaining silence. Preferably, for each circuit, you should blow your spirit through the keyhole of the church door. Returning home towards morning, you would then sense in various ways what the coming year had in store.

Christmas Day was usually celebrated very quietly indeed. No unnecessary work was permitted. The Christmas table was left laid during Christmas night, so that the meal could be continued where people had left off, without any extra work in the kitchen. There were also those who believed that the food should be left out for dead relatives during the magical night preceding Christmas.

But before this Christmas calm descended, the early morning service beckoned. "People were up and about early on Christmas morning. Father would be given a glass of bitters and bread and cheese in bed. The other men would also come in for bitters, bread and cheese before going off to the shippon. There you weren't allowed to muck out, and after you'd done what absolutely had to be done, you put on your best clothes and drove to the early morning service,"

somebody from Andrarum recalls.

Early meant just that, but not so early as to risk horning in on the Christmas morning service of the dead. This preceded the regular service and was attended by the dead of the parish, who rose from their graves and sat down in the pews like ordinary churchgoers. That is why, sometimes, the crunching of gravel and soil could be heard in the pews when the real service was going on. If you happened to intrude on the earlier service, the thing was to leave the church quickly, silently and undiscovered. The story goes of a woman who managed this by the skin of her teeth, making off in such a hurry that she dropped her coat. A couple of hours later, when the real service was about to start, the churchgoers found fragments of the coat on every grave.

The Christmas Table

HERRING PLATE

INGREDIENTS:
1 kg fillets of salt herring soaked and drained

PICKLING LIQUID:
2 l. water
3 tbsp. vinegar (24% *ättika* – distilled vinegar)
2 dl sugar

PICKLE 1:
1 l. water
1 1/2 tbsp. *ättika*
1 dl sugar
1 tbsp. caraway
1 dl concentrated apple juice
1 or 2 apples

PICKLE 2:
1 can of crushed tomatoes
1 pot or bunch of basil
1 or 2 cloves of garlic

PICKLE 3:
6 cl Skåne Akvavit schnapps
1 fennel bulb
1 or 2 star anise

PROCEDURE:
For any "herring plate", of course, the choice of pickling recipes is yours alone. I have chosen three which, to my mind, have typically Scanian flavours. You can start by making a pickling liquid in which you put all the fillets of herring after you have finished soaking and draining them. Here they stay for at least 24 hours. (A lot of old recipes use whole herring, not fillets, because in many people's opinion, the bones give added flavour to the pickling liquid. "Glazier's Herring", for example, and the typically Scanian "spiced herring" are always made using whole herring on the bone.)
It then only remains to add whatever flavourings you fancy.
The herring should be left in its flavouring for at least three days, for the spices to do their job. If a pickle has "faded" a lot at the end of that time, the spices may need reinforcing.
And that, really, is just about all there is to it. You make the pickling liquid by mixing a litre of water with 3 tbsp. *ättika* and 2 dl sugar. You needn't warm it, so long as you stir everything thoroughly enough to dissolve all the sugar. Make quite sure, you can bring the mixture to the boil. Some cooks insist on this, but then you lose time waiting for the liquid to cool again before you can add the herring to it. Personally I see no need for boiling the liquid.

SPICE LIQUID 1:
Mix a new liquid of the same strength as the first and flavour with 1 tbsp. caraway, 1 dl concentrated apple juice and 1 or 2 apples, chipped fine with the peel on but de-cored. Remove the herring from the first liquid, transfer it to the spiced liquid and let it stand for at least three days.

SPICE LIQUID 2:
Mix 1 can of crushed tomatoes with 1 pot/bunch fresh basil. Press two cloves of garlic into this and mix. Insert the herring fillets and include a little of the first liquid for extra sweetness and sharpness. Leave for at least three days.

SPICE LIQUID 3:
Make up a liquid the same as the first, but this time flavour it with 6 cl Skåne Akvavit schnapps, 1 fennel bulb chopped fine and 2-3 stars of anise. Remove the herring from the first liquid, transfer to this one and leave for at least three days.

A pukka "herring plate" should be garnished with a few halves of boiled egg and served with steaming hot, fresh-boiled potatoes.

TROTTERS AND TAILS

Serves 4

INGREDIENTS:
4 pigs' trotters
1 carrot
1 parsnip
1 onion
2 tbsp. salt
5 corns of white pepper
allspice
bay leaves
4 pigs' tails
butter for frying

PROCEDURE:
1. Clean the trotters very thoroughly indeed. The easiest way is with a nailbrush under the cold tap.
2. Peel and dice the root vegetables and the onion.
3. Bring some lightly salted water to the boil. Put in the trotters and let them keep boiling for a minute or so.
4. Drain and then rinse the trotters in cold water. Refill the saucepan with water, inserting the diced vegetables and onion with the trotters. Add the salt and spices and cook for about 30 minutes over a gentle flame.
5. Transfer to bowls with the water and either serve immediately or leave the trotters to cool overnight so that they can be eaten cold with the jelly of the water and vegetables.
6. Clean the pigs' tails in the same way as the trotters, but instead of boiling them, fry them in butter. 10 minutes or so will do, and then add salt and pepper.
7. Cut up in small pieces for serving.

BRÄNNESNUDA

Serves 4

INGREDIENTS:
2 carrots
1 parsnip
2 celeriac bulbs
2 or 3 potatoes
1.2–2 kg lightly salted loin of pork
1 or 2 bay leaves
2 or 3 corns of allspice
1 or 2 corns of white pepper
1/2 head of white cabbage
1 bunch of parsley
1 leek

PROCEDURE:

1. Peel the root vegetables and cut them in small pieces.
2. Bring the meat to the boil in plenty of water, together with the spices and root vegetables. Skim and then cook for another hour or so or until the meat is done, i.e. has an inner temperature of at least 70°C.
3. Chop the cabbage, parsley and leek and add them towards the end.
4. Slice the pork and serve it with the stock and all the green vegetables.

EGG CAKE

Serves 4

INGREDIENTS:

About 400 g lightly salted pork or, better still, smoked pork (2 or 3 slices per person)
2 dl white flour
3 dl milk
1 tbsp. sugar
1 tsp. salt
1 dl double cream
3 eggs
To serve: chopped chives and coarse salt

PROCEDURE:

1. Cut the pork into thick slices.
2. Beat the flour and milk to a smooth batter.
3. Beat in the sugar, salt, cream and eggs.
4. Fry the pork in a cast iron pan with a tall, straight rim.
5. Remove the pork when ready and keep it warm while slowly frying the egg cake, in the fat from the pork, on a low to medium flame. Cover. When the cake has turned a nice colour, use the cover to turn it over so that you can fry the other side as well.
6. Serve the egg cake with the pork and a little fine-chopped chives and coarse salt.

The Christmas Table

COLLARED BRAWN SMOKED CHRISTMAS HAM AND FRIED CABBAGE

COLLARED BRAWN

INGREDIENTS:
lightly salted side of pork
Skåne mustard
freshly milled white pepper
ground allspice
kitchen string

IN THE BOILING WATER
1/2 tbsp. *ättika* (Swedish distilled vinegar)
1 or 2 cloves
2 or 3 bay leaves
5 or 6 corns of allspice

PROCEDURE:
1. Spread mustard on the pork and scatter a little fresh-milled white pepper and allspice over it. Roll up and tie with string in several places. At this stage you may need an extra pair of hands to hold everything together while you are tying the knots.

2. Now boil the meat, in just enough water to cover it, and with the lid on, for about 2 hours/kilo.
3. Remove the meat and put it under pressure so that it will keep its shape after it has cooled.
4. Serve cold and thinly sliced.

CHRISTMAS HAM

Most people nowadays, presumably, buy their ham ready-cooked. Sugar-salted in most parts of the country, or sugar-salted and lightly smoked, as here in Skåne. If you are doing your own, start by sugar-salting. This calls for a special tool to guarantee that the brine penetrates properly. This brine consists of saltpetre and sugar mixed with water. The smoking of the ham is a chapter in itself.

FRIED CABBAGE

The most Scanian of Christmas cabbages!

INGREDIENTS:
1 head of white cabbage
cooking fat for frying
5 dl treacle
salt, pepper

PROCEDURE:
1. Cut away the stalk and the outer leaves and make strips of the rest.
2. Melt a little fat in a big saucepan and pour in the cabbage. Simmer on a medium to high flame, stirring all the time. When the cabbage begins to darken and soften a little, pour on the treacle and flavour with salt and pepper.
3. Lower the temperature and leave the cabbage to simmer on a gentle flame for about 30 minutes. Stir every now and again, to keep it from sticking. Check the flavour.
4. When you are satisfied with the flavour and appearance of the cabbage, that's it. Remove it from the heat and leave it to cool on a big tray, stew pan or suchlike. Leave it in the fridge for a day or two, and the flavour will ripen still further.
5. Serve warm together with the ham.

SCANIAN "CRÈME CARAMEL"

with a cinnamon-flavoured caramel sauce

Serves 4

INGREDIENTS:
6 eggs
1 apple
1 l. full-cream milk or 1/2 l. cream + 1/2 l. milk
3 tbsp. sugar
peel of 1 lemon

CARAMEL SAUCE:
4 tbsp. water
about 3 dl sugar
a pinch or so of cinnamon

PROCEDURE:
CARAMEL SAUCE:
1. Boil the water in a saucepan.
2. Melt the sugar in a frying pan, dilute the melted butter with 3 tbsp. of the boiling water. Carefully add a little cinnamon, stirring continually.
3. Pour the caramel sauce into the mould/s you intend using and dust with the ground cinnamon (preferably through a tea strainer).
4. Beat the eggs (the best way is by parting them, beating the whites first and then adding the yolks).
5. Peel and de-core the apple and chop it as fine as you can.
6. Boil the milk with the sugar, the fine-chopped apple and the grated lemon peel. Leave to cool slightly, then add the beaten eggs.
7. Pour the mixture into the "glazed" mould/s. Bake in a bain-marie in the oven at 175°C for about 45 minutes.
8. Put to cool in the fridge. When the pudding is quite cold it can be turned out. Try serving this with slices of apple fried in sugar and cinnamon.

Christmas fun and games

Christmas day was a quiet family occasion, but on Boxing Day the festivities and the fun and games began. Somebody from Albo recalls: "On the morning of Boxing Day you had to be up early to receive those who came to sing the song of St Stephen. If you weren't up, the singers might drag the manure into the shippon. At every farm where they sang, one more rider had to join them. This was mostly a day for going out and calling on each other. Young people got together in groups for fun and games."

In the "Stephen's ride" farm lads and farmers' sons got together and rode from farm to farm, singing and importuning. Their aim was to collect enough food and drink for their festivities between Christmas and the New Year.

Most people in Sweden know the song of St Stephen (*Staffansvisan*) but perhaps the legend behind it is less familiar. At the time when Jesus was born, King Herod had a stablehand called Stefanos. Suddenly one winter's night, Stefanos saw the Star of Bethlehem light up in the heavens. He immediately understood what this meant and told Herod that a king, mightier even than he was, had just been born. Herod was furious and had the stable boy stoned to death, making Stefanos the first Christian martyr. As such, his feast day was appointed for the day after the birth of Christ, 26th December.

The village Christmas feast conformed to a special roster among the participants. Usually these parties were for married couples with very young children. The young people had another type of festivity, called "Christmas cottages", at which they decked the table with food, beer and

Stephen's Ride. Drawing by August Ehrenberg.

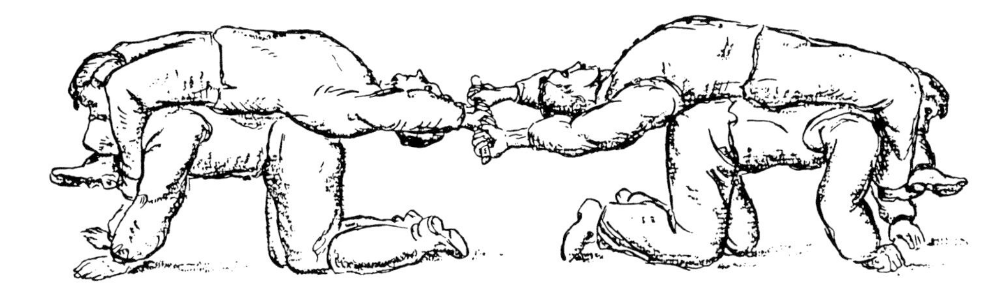

"Pulling the Ox" was a popular game during Christmas festivities.

schnapps baked previously. There would also be dancing if they could get hold of a fiddler. And there were games of different kinds. Those for the boys were often trials of strength and balance, such as "Pulling the Ox", a kind of two-aside tug-of-war, or "Smack Markus", in which blind-folded combatants struck out at each other with knotted towels. The girls' games were usually quieter forfeit or guessing games in which the object was to form couples.

Olof Rudbeck describes some of these games in his book *Atlantica*, published at the end of the 17th century: "All our Christmas games divided our ancestors into two teams, as is also the case today, with men's games and maids' games. The men's games are quite rough even today, with many people sustaining black eyes and broken arms and legs, though not so much as formerly. The games nowadays are: Pinch a Steak, Blind Man's Buff, Mussel my Shoe, Taming Steers, Drying Malt, Riding to the King, Bumming the Pitchfork, Neck and Neck, Guess Who Hit You, Let us Meet and then be Beat, Mark and Luke, Sailing to Germany, Stand in the Bucket, Creeping to the Cross and many others in which blows are dealt, though in moderation."

"Mark and Luke" lives on as "Are you there, Moriarty?"

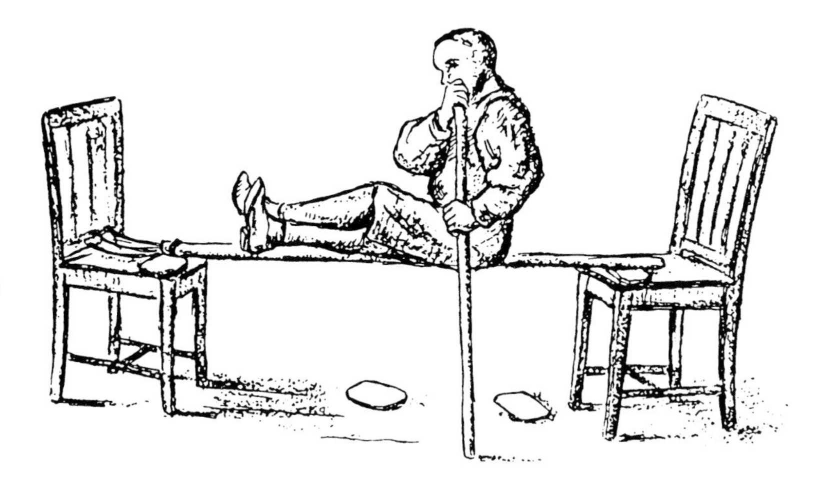

"Bumming the Pitchfork" was a real test of balance and agility.

Red-letter days early in the year

New Year in the old agrarian society was another quiet family occasion. People ate and drank what was left of their Christmas fare. Lobster and champagne are a middle-class invention which only became widely current in the 20th century.

The New Year was also significant to country folk, though, marking as it did the transition from something old to something new. Markings of this kind have always been credited with a special, often magical significance. There were traditionally believed to be powerful forces in motion on New Year's Eve, and to frighten away the nasty ones the men would often fire a couple of gunshots into the blackness of the night.

But people also wished to benefit from the magical power of the stroke of midnight by trying to look into the future. They cast lead, recorded the weather on New Year's Eve (a windy night portended a windy year to come) and they studied the fruit trees (if the odd winter apple still remained on the tree, it would be a good year for the crops). There were even dodges for controlling the future. One of them was to give cows and horses an extra meal of hay and oats on the evening of New Year's Eve. That way they would stay healthy and strong all through the coming year.

The Bible tells us that it took the Three Wise Men - Caspar, Melchior and Balthazar – 13 days to find their way to the Christ Child in Bethlehem. And so *The Thirteenth Day*, as we call it in Sweden, is celebrated on 6th January and in Denmark is still known as "The Three Kings' Day". Right down to the present, the Danes have celebrated the day with pranks and dressing up.

The fact is that the "Starboys" in the Lucia procession can also be traced back to the Epiphany, because old biblical tradition made them a guard of honour and retinue to the Three Wise Men. They can also be said to be related to the Stephen Riders - farmers' sons and farmhands who, on Boxing Day, rode from farm to farm, singing and begging food and schnapps.

Twenty days after Christmas we celebrate *Twenty-day Knut*, 13th January (Hilarymas). Tradition had it that Knut must drive out Christmas (and the Christmas guests), the reference being to King Knut Lavard of Denmark, who was basely murdered on that day (7th January according to the old calendar) in Ringsted, Denmark. His memory is perpetuated in the Knut Guilds surviving from medieval times in Denmark and in some formerly Danish parts of Sweden, such as Lund, Malmö, Thumatorp (Tomarp) and Visby.

In Skåne in olden days, "Knut men" used to be given away on Knut's Day or, especially in the south-eastern part of the province, Felix men on Felix Day, which comes after it. These were straw dolls, often with some ribald greeting attached.

The real *Candlemas* comes on 2nd February, but in our modern calendars it has been moved to the nearest Sunday. It commemorates the Purification of the Virgin, 40 days after Christmas. For this reason it used to be common for women who had given birth in December to be churched on this day. Candlemas, then, is the last red-letter day in the calendar that has anything to do with Christmas.

SCANIAN NEW YEAR MENU

Starter: Goose liver, prune and apple starter served with a Sauternes sauce

Serves 4

INGREDIENTS:
1 bag of stoneless prunes
3 tbsp. sugar
3 leaves of gelatine
1 jar of *pâté de foie gras* (bought ready-made for convenience, but otherwise see the recipe below)
1 or 2 apples
2 dl Sauternes (or Tokay)
salt, pepper
cornflour

PROCEDURE:
For this recipe you need a round cutter and a mixer.
1. Put the prunes and sugar in a saucepan and cover them with water.
2. Soften the leaves of gelatine in cold water and put them in the pot as well.
3. Bring to the boil and then remove from the heat. Mix with a stick blender or run in the food processor to a fairly smooth consistency.
4. Spread the mixture on a baking tray lined with grease-proof paper and then leave in the fridge until it has set completely.
5. Cut equal-sized rounds of the *pâté de foie gras* and the prune mixture.
6. Peel the apples, cut them in slices of equal thickness and then from these slices cut out rounds the same size as before.
7. Make a tower of all the rounds and encircle with decorative herbal oils, such as raspberry oil or beetroot oil. You can easily make these yourself by blending, say, raspberries (frozen or fresh), a herb or a little beetroot/yellow beet, together with ordinary cooking oil.
8. SAUCE: Bring the Sauternes to the boil and thicken with the cornflour.

PÂTÉ DE FOIE GRAS

INGREDIENTS:
2 dl Madeira
200 g butter
200 g goose liver
1 clove of garlic (optional)
1 pinch of saltpetre
1 pinch of sugar
salt, pepper

PROCEDURE:
For this recipe you need a food processor or mixer and an oblong, oven-proof mould.
1. Begin by reducing the Madeira by at least half or still more. Leave to cool.
2. Melt the butter and leave this to cool slightly as well.
3. Line the oven-proof mould with heat-proof cling foil or greased baking tray paper.
4. Mix the liver with the spices and, still mixing, add the melted butter without the residue of water. Keep the mixer running and add the Madeira.
5. Pour the mixture into the mould and bake in the oven in a bain-marie at 175°C for about an hour or until the pâté has completely settled. Put to cool in the fridge for at least 12 hours.

SCANIAN NEW YEAR MENU

Main course: Cod pastry with lobster, zucchini and paprika, served with a champagne sauce

Serves 4

INGREDIENTS:
1 orange, red or yellow paprika
1 large zucchini
800 g. fillet of cod (preferably scaled, but not skinned)
2 whole boiled lobsters
cooking oil
salt, pepper
(Optional: 1 or 2 large baked potatoes to go with it)

SAUCE:
onion
cooking fat for frying
1–2 dl fish stock (your own or from a cube)
1–2 dl champagne (or suchlike)
5 dl double cream
arrowroot or cornflour stirred into water, for thickening
salt, pepper

PROCEDURE:
This time you need a grill or – less trouble, perhaps in winter – a grill pan.
1. Prepare the paprika by dividing it into relatively large pieces and removing the core.
2. Cut the zucchini into centimetre-thick slices.
3. Fry the pieces of paprika quickly in the frying pan, so that you can peel them easily.
4. Cut the fish into suitably sized pieces, so as to give at least 3 or 4 pieces per person. Now cut up the lobster, so that everyone gets two bits of the tail and a claw.
5. Now heat the grill or the grill pan as high as possible, so that it really smokes. Meanwhile turn the pieces of fish and lobster on kitchen tissue to get rid of the surplus liquid and then brush them with just a little cooking oil. Scatter on a little salt as well.
6. Grill the pieces of paprika, the slices of zucchini and the pieces of fish and lobster. (If you like, you can also use centimetre-thick slices of baked potato.) When everything is nicely patterned, transfer to greaseproof paper in a roasting tin and put this in a warming cabinet or in the oven at minimum temperature. Leave everything there while you are making the sauce.
7. Make an ordinary white wine sauce by first chopping the onion and "melting" this in a casserole with just a little fat. Pour on the fish stock and half the champagne. Reduce slightly and then pour on the cream. Leave the sauce to stand and boil until it starts thickening a little.
8. Before serving, bring the sauce to the boil again and pour on the rest of the champagne.
9. Now comes the "balancing act" of making all the different parts into a small tower-shape composition – anathema to the trendies.
Time permitting, fluff the sauce a little extra with a stick blender before serving and wriggle it round the tower.

SCANIAN NEW YEAR MENU

Dessert:
Cinnamon and aniseed-flavoured vanilla mousse with an orange and glögg sorbet

Serves 4

INGREDIENTS:
5 oranges
about 4 dl *glögg* (Swedish mulled wine)
5 dl double cream
1 vanilla pod
1/2 dl sugar
2 stars of anise
1 stick of cinnamon
4 leaves of gelatine

PROCEDURE:
This dish is most conveniently made in an ice cream machine. (You can do it without, but in that case you have to stir the sorbet at regular intervals after you have put it in the freezer, until it is set almost completely.)

1. SORBET: Wash the oranges and grate the peel. Divide and press the oranges, and pour the juice and the grated peel into an ice cream machine.
2. Pour about 4 dl concentrated *glögg* into the ice cream machine. Stir a little, to mix the ingredients, and check the strength. If you find the mixture too strong, add a little water. (Remember, though, that sorbets and ice cream don't have such a strong flavour after chilling.)
3. MOUSSE: Pour the cream into a pot, split a vanilla pod down the middle, scrape the contents into the pot and add the cinnamon stick.
4. Pour in the sugar, star of anise and cinnamon stick and cook gently for 10 or 15 minutes. Remove the vanilla pod, the cinnamon stick and the star of anise.
5. Dissolve the leaves of gelatine in a little cold water. When they have softened (after about 5 minutes) remove them, wring out the water and put them in the pot. Stir until the leaves are completely dissolved by the heat and then pour the mousse into 4 small china bowls, coffee cups or suchlike. Leave in the fridge until fully set.
6. Serve the mousse with the sorbet.

PARSNIP SOUP

with smoked pork and parsley

Serves 4

INGREDIENTS:

About 250 g parsnips
5 dl milk
5 dl double cream
salt, pepper
200 g smoked pork, diced
1 small bunch parsley

PROCEDURE:

For this recipe you need a mixer or food processor.

1. Peel the parsnips and cut them into small pieces.
2. Boil the pieces in milk until they have softened a little (about 5 minutes).
3. Pour everything into a mixer/food processor and run until smooth.

N.B. Don't fill right up to the top – do it by stages. This way, if the mixture turns out too thick and lumpy, you can add more cream.

4. Return the smooth, creamy soup to the pot and add to it any cream that may be left over. If there is none left, you can use milk or even water to get the right consistency.
5. Add salt and pepper to taste.

Remember that both cream and root vegetables need quite a generous dose of salt. Now remove the soup from the heat for the time being.

6. Heat a frying pan and frizzle the diced pork without any cooking fat. Meanwhile you can also chop the parsley – as fine as possible.

7. Bring the soup to the boil one last time before serving it, and then tip in the diced pork and the chopped parsley.

COOK'S COMMENT

This was an attempt to demonstrate continental links which, of course have always been a distinctive quality of Scanian food. Our next-door neighbour to the south gave me the idea of imitating what the Germans call "imperial potato soup". Personally, though, I feel that substituting the Swedish parsnip for the humble potato adds an even more "imperial" touch. An easy, quick soup if you're looking for a starter or a simple dinner.

SALT-BAKED ARTICHOKES

on a bed of black radish preserve and citrus fillets

Serves 4

INGREDIENTS:

12 Jerusalem artichokes
1 black radish
1 dl sugar
2 tbsp. 24% *ättika* (Swedish distilled vinegar)
2–3 dl coarse salt
1 lemon
1 grapefruit (blood grapefruit if possible)
1 orange

PROCEDURE:

1. Peel the artichokes and black radish. Make thin strips of the black radish.
2. Bring to the boil a mixture of the sugar, about 2 dl water and the *ättika*. Add the shredded radish and boil for 3 or 5 minutes. Leave the whole thing to cool.
3. Pour out the coarse salt in an oven-proof dish and put the peeled artichokes on it. Bake in the oven at 150°C for about 5 minutes.
4. Meanwhile you can peel all the citrus fruits and cut out clean wedges.
5. Arrange the wedges nicely on the plate. Make a pile of the sweet-and-sour radish strips with the artichokes on top. If you feel like it, mix a fresh herb with oil and pour this over the whole thing. A quick, easy and rather unusual starter, this one.

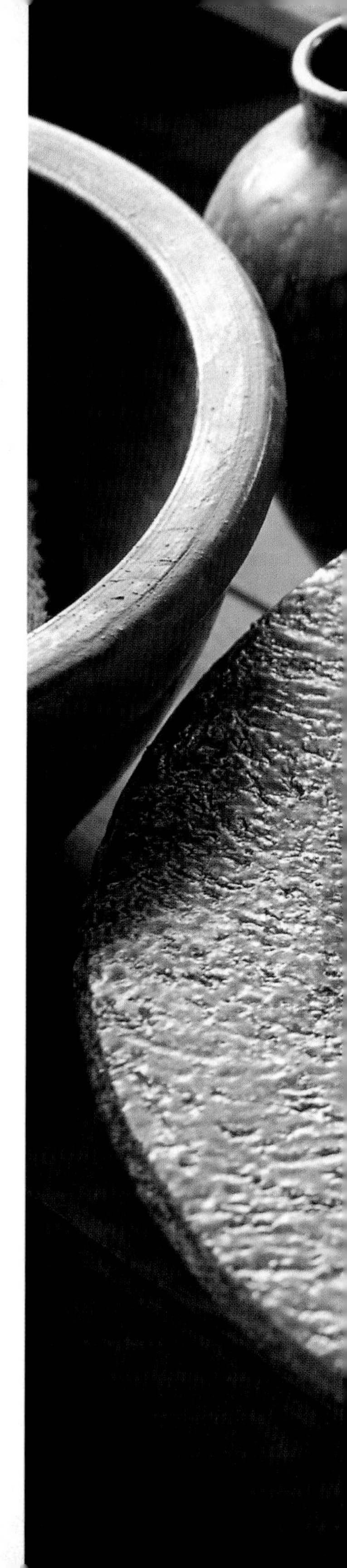

THYME-FLAVOURED SALT HERRING WITH A RYE BREAD COATING

served with coated apple slices and a potato vinaigrette

Serves 4

INGREDIENTS:
1 medium sized potato
1 big apple
1 dl flour
1 pinch of dried thyme
2 dl dried breadcrumbs, preferably rye bread
1 egg
4 fillets of salt herring, soaked and drained
1/2 dl cooking oil
1 tbsp. white wine vinegar
1 tsp. good mustard
salt, pepper
1 bunch of herbs (dill, parsley or chives)
cooking fat for frying

Serve with a good salad.

PROCEDURE:
1. Peel and boil the potato. Let it disintegrate if you like, because you're going to mash it anyway.
2. Split the apple, remove the core and slice the halves.
3. Pour out the flour, mixed with thyme, on one plate, the dried breadcrumbs on a second plate and the egg, beaten in 2 or 3 tbsp. water, on a third.
4. Double-coat the herring fillets (thoroughly soaked and de-salted) and the slices of apple by turning them first in the flour, then in the egg and lastly in the breadcrumbs.
5. Mash the potato when it's ready. You can very well use the cooking water for thinning out the mash, to give it a viscous consistency.
6. Stir in the oil and flavour with vinegar, a touch of mustard (remember that mustard thickens liquid) and salt and pepper. Chop in a little parsley, dill or chives for a nice green colour.
7. Fry the coated slices of apple and pieces of herring in the frying pan with a little fat, perhaps on a slightly lower flame, to rule out the risk of any "burnt offering".
8. Serve on a bed of lettuce with the potato vinaigrette.

"TOUSLED" SALAD OF RAW VEGETABLES

with strips of Scanian "spickeskinka" and a Scanian/Indonesian dressing

Serves 4

INGREDIENTS:
2 medium-sized carrots
1 medium-sized parsnip
1 medium-sized parsley root (aka Hamburg parsley)
1/2 kohlrabi
1/2 black radish
1/2 celeriac
about 100 g "spickeskinka", thinly sliced (salted and cold smoked ham)
1 apple
1 dl stewed apple
1/2 dl Ketjap Manis (Indonesian sweet soy)
coarse salt/sea salt

PROCEDURE:
1. Peel and grate all the root vegetables to strips. Strip the slices of ham as well.
2. De-core the apple and chop small.
3. Mix everything thoroughly in a bowl.
4. Mix the stewed apple and soya in a small bowl.
5. To serve, place a slightly "tousled" pile of the raw vegetable salad and ham in the middle of the plate and then pour the dark, viscous dressing round it.

COOK'S COMMENT

The really distinctive characteristic of Scanian food has been its amenability to foreign influence. Here is a perfect example of the mingling of flavours, the typical Scanian apple with the Asian sweet-salt soy. Also the perfect appetiser – a pointer to the Scanian menu.

TJÄLKNÖL FILLET OF VENISON

Serves 10–15

INGREDIENS:

1 1/2–2 kg deep-frozen venison steak (preferably inner fillet)
potatoes of a floury kind (King Edward, for example), 200–250 g per person

SAUCE

marinade
venison stock or a stock cube
double cream (optional)
1 onion

MARINADE

1 l. small beer
1 dl red wine vinegar
2 dl cooking oil
1 tbsp. sugar
1–2 bunches of fresh rosemary (or 2 pinches of the dried version)
5–6 bunches of fresh thyme (or 2–3 pinches dried)
3 crushed juniper berries
salt, pepper

PROCEDURE:

1. First of all, put the "lump of ground frost" (that's what the name means) in the oven on a rack (preferably with a roasting pan underneath, to collect all the juices) and roast at 70°C for at least 8 or 12 hours. (Overnight is the best way.) For a perfectly pink steak, the inner temperature should be between 55 and 65°C. Use a meat thermometer. This can be inserted in the meat after 6 or 7 hours.
2. When the steak is ready, put it straight into a marinade. (See suggested recipe, above.) Leave it there for at least 3 or 4 hours, turning it occasionally so that the flavour soaks right in.
3. Remove the steak and dry it thoroughly.
4. You could very well use some of the marinade to make a sauce. Mix the marinade with fine-chopped onion and a little venison stock (or a stock cube dissolved in 5 dl boiling water). Reduce thoroughly, add salt and pepper to taste.
5. Serve in thin slices, with the sauce and one or two boiled potatoes.

SALT-BAKED ENTRECÔTE OF VEAL

with root vegetable strips baked in parsley

Serves 4

INGREDIENTS:

500 g coarse or gourmet salt
about 600 g veal entrecôte
2 large carrots
2 parsnips
2 parsley roots
1/2 celeriac
1 small bunch of parsley
1 tbsp. oil
1 dl veal stock
1/2 dl red wine

PROCEDURE:

1. Make the coarse salt into a salt dough by running it in a mixer with 1 or 2 tbsp. water. This takes quite a long time. If necessary, add more water after a while. N.B. It's easy to overdo the water, so go easy!
2. Plaster the dough all over the meat and bake in the oven at 200°C for 20 or 30 minutes or till the dough has turned a nice colour.
3. Meanwhile peel the root vegetables and cut them into strips measuring about 1 x 5 cm.
4. Chop the parsley and roll the strips first in the oil and then in the parsley choppings.
5. Put the root vegetables in to fry with the meat for the last 5 minutes or until they have turned a nice colour. Break and discard the salt crust.
6. Dilute the veal stock with a dash of wine and a dash of water to a nice flavour and serve with meat.
7. Slice the entrecôte and serve with the sauce and root vegetables. A good, lean dinner!

COOK'S COMMENT

There is nothing new about baking meat in salt dough, but it could never have been done further north in Sweden, because salt there was much harder to come by. And there is really no need to throw away the salt after using it with the meat - if only you can find a second use for it!

PRUNE SOUFFLÉ

with orange sauce and raspberry sauce

Serves 8–10

INGREDIENTS:
1 1/2 –2 dl stoned prunes
unsalted butter for greasing the mould
1 dl sugar (+ about 1/2 dl sugar for the moulds)
6 large egg whites (about 3 dl)

ORANGE SAUCE:
5 oranges
1 dl sugar (or according to taste)
water (according to taste)
cornflour, arrowroot or potato flour for thickening

RASPBERRY SAUCE:
2 dl raspberries
1/2 dl red wine
1/2 dl sugar
1/2 dl water

PROCEDURE:
For this recipe you need a mixer or food processor.
1. Set the oven to 150°C. Boil the prunes for about 5 minutes in a little water. Drain and leave to cool a little.
2. Butter and sugar 8–10 oven-proof ramekins.
3. Run the prunes in the mixer/food processor to a paste. This needn't be perfectly smooth.
4. Beat the egg whites in sugar stiff. Mix with the prune paste.
5. Pour the mixture into the ramekins and bake in the oven in a bain-marie for about 25 minutes.
6. Meanwhile, make a simple raspberry sauce by running raspberries, red wine, sugar and water in a mixer. You could strain off the pips by putting the sauce through a fine sieve or strainer.
7. Make an orange sauce too, by juicing the oranges after first washing and grating the peel. (Remove the pips.)
8. Bring the orange juice and peel to the boil together with the sugar and 1–1 1/2 dl water in a saucepan. Thicken with cornflour, arrowroot or potato flour, dissolved in a little cold water, to the required consistency.
9. If your ambition is to present nice fluffy soufflés, you must serve them straight from the oven. But they are just as good and less hassle when served cold. In this case, turn off the oven but leave the ramekins in for another 20 minutes or so. Put the soufflés in the fridge to cool thoroughly and serve them when it suits you.

COOK'S COMMENT

Oranges may not be Scanian, but all the other ingredients are. Serving this dessert cold will spare you the jitters of perfectionism.

NOUGAT PANNACOTTA

with a citrus salad flavoured with star anise and vanilla

Serves 4

INGREDIENTS:

2 leaves of gelatine
2 vanilla pods
5 dl double cream
1 1/2 dl sugar
100 g soft nougat (e.g. Odense)
1 dl sweet almonds and hazel nuts, mixed
2 tbsp. honey
2 oranges
2 grapefruit (blood grapefruit, preferably)
2 limes
1 lemon
3–4 star anises

PROCEDURE:

1. Soak the gelatine in cold water.
2. Split a vanilla pod down the middle and scrape the seeds into a saucepan.
3. Boil the cream, 1/2 dl sugar and the vanilla seeds for about 10 minutes.
4. Add the soft nougat and stir until it has melted completely.
5. When the gelatine leaves have softened, remove them, wring out the water and add them to the nougat mixture. Stir and remove from the heat.
6. Chop the nuts and almonds as fine as possible.
7. Pour the honey into a frying pan, add the chopped nuts and almonds and stir, over a relatively high flame, with a wooden spoon. Pour all this into the mixture and then transfer to ramekins (coffee cups will do). Put in the fridge to set.
8. Peel the citrus fruits, slice them and put them in a bowl.
9. Boil a syrup of 1 dl sugar, 3 dl water and 3 or 4 star anises.
10. Split the other vanilla pod down the middle and scrape the contents into the syrup. Reduce by half.
11. Pour the syrup over the slices of fruit and leave for as long as possible before serving (preferably 1 or 2 days).
12. Turn up the pannacottas after loosening them all round with a small knife. Serve with the cirrus salad.

MOCHA MOUSSE

with punch cream and citrus cream

Serves 4

INGREDIENTS:

About 1 cup of ready-brewed coffee
8 egg yolks
7 or 8 tbsp. sugar
2 tbsp. punch (Swedish arrack if possible)
1 dl double cream
1 orange
1 grapefruit (blood grapefruit preferably)
1 lime
2 dl crème fraîche

PROCEDURE:

MOCHA MOUSSE

1. Pour the coffee into a saucepan and reduce by just over half.
2. Beat 4 egg yolks in 2 tbsp. sugar to a thick, fluffy consistency. Use an electric whisk.
3. Add the reduced coffee and whisk together. Add more sugar to taste, if you like.

PUNCH CREAM

1. Pour 2 tbsp. punch, 2 tbsp. sugar and 4 egg yolks into a saucepan and beat continuously over a gentle flame (perhaps in a bain-marie) to a thick, fluffy consistency. Leave to cool.
2. Whisk 1 dl double cream and mix this with the cold punch mixture. Add more punch and/or sugar if you like.

CITRUS CREAM

1. Wash the citrus fruits and grate the peel into a saucepan.
2. Divide the fruit and juice it. Pour the juice into the saucepan.
3. Add the crème fraîche and 3 tbsp. sugar. Bring to the boil, stirring continuously. Remove from the heat and leave to cool.
4. Transfer alternate layers of mocha mousse, punch cream and citrus cream to four tall glasses.

CHERRIES MARINATED IN SHERRY

with cream of white chocolate, lemon balm and vanilla ice cream

Serves 4

INGREDIENTS:

1 or 2 vanilla pods (depending on size and quality)
1 l. + 3 tbsp. full cream milk
5 dl sugar
8 + 4 egg yolks
about 25 cherries
2 dl sweet sherry
1 pot/bunch of lemon balm
1 or 2 tsp. potato flour for thickening
1 dl white wine
200 g white chocolate

PROCEDURE:

For this recipe you need a mixer or food processor. For the ice cream you need an ice-cream machine.

1. Start by making the ice cream. Split the vanilla pod down the middle and scrape the seeds into a saucepan. Pour on 1 l. full cream milk and 4 dl sugar and bring to the boil. Remove from the heat and leave to cool.
2. Beat 8 of the egg yolks to a thick liquid which you then mix with the vanilla and full cream milk.
3. Run the mixture in an ice-cream machine. When it is set, transfer it to a suitable bowl for temporary storage in the freezer. (Cop-out: buy your vanilla ice cream ready-made.)
4. Divide and stone the cherries. Warm the sherry and pour in 1/2 dl sugar. Stir until the sugar dissolves. Add the cherries. Store in the fridge, preferably until next day.
5. LEMON BALM SAUCE: Pour about 2 dl water into a mixer or food processor, plus as many of the lemon balm leaves as you like and 1/2 dl sugar. Mix together, transfer to a saucepan and bring to the boil.
6. Make a thickening with a little potato flour stirred in water. When the sauce boils, strain the thickening into it carefully, stirring all the time. Put the sauce in the fridge to cool thoroughly.

7. WHITE CHOCOLATE CREAM: Pour the wine into a stainless saucepan with 4 egg yolks and beat over a gentle flame. Beat carefully all over the bottom of the saucepan without a break, so the mixture doesn't curdle. Keep going until the yolks are thick and fluffy.
8. Divide the white chocolate in small pieces and stir them in the egg sauce to give a smooth mixture. Pour in 3 tbsp. cream to thin the sauce a little. Leave to cool.
9. Put the marinated cherries on plates together with the ice cream and both sauces.

AN EASY CHOCOLATE CAKE FOR THE MULTITUDE

INGREDIENTS:
8 eggs
500 g dark cooking chocolate
500 g butter (preferably unsalted)
500 g icing sugar
1 tbsp. ground cardamom
4 1/2 dl sifted rye flour
white chocolate or icing sugar for garnish (optional)

PROCEDURE:
1. Separate the yolks from the whites.
2. Melt the chocolate and butter in a saucepan over a low flame. Stir in the icing sugar and cardamom. Make sure the sugar melts properly. Stir continuously with a wooden spoon, so nothing sticks.
3. Stir in the flour, followed by the yolks.
4. Beat the egg whites stiff and stir them in as well.
5. Grease a roasting tray or line it with baking tray paper and then spread out the mixture over this.
6. Bake in the oven at 175–200°C for 20 minutes. Transfer to the fridge until thoroughly cooled.
7. Garnish by trailing melted white chocolate over the top or dusting it with a little icing sugar. Cut into squares and serve.

OUR DAILY BREAD

Rye bread

(possibly in sourdough form)
4 loaves

INGREDIENTS:
60 g (just over 1 packet) yeast
5 dl lukewarm (37°C) water
1 pinch salt
1 1/2 dl lingonberry jam
600 g (10–11 dl) sifted rye flower
400 g (about 6 1/2 dl) white flour
1 dl roasted sunflower seeds

PROCEDURE:
1. Dissolve the yeast in the lukewarm water. Add the salt and lingonberry jam.
2. Run the flour, sunflower seeds and liquid in a food processor. The dough is rather sticky, so flour your hands before trying to get it out of the mixing bowl.
3. Divide the dough in four pieces and shape them into loaves. Put these on a baking tray lined with baking tray paper or into greased loaf tins. Leave to rise for 1/2–1 hour.
4. Bake the loaves at 175°C in the middle of the oven for about 20 minutes.

COOK'S/BAKER'S COMMENT
For the real Häckeberga Wärdshus flavour, you need a sourdough. Substitute part of that for the yeast.

Coarse bread

2 loaves

INGREDIENTS:
9 dl white flour
9 dl sifted rye flour
2 dl crushed rye
5 tsp. baking powder
5 tsp. bicarbonate
1 l. soured milk
2 1/2 dl treacle

PROCEDURE:
1. Mix all the dry ingredients in a food processor for 2 or 3 minutes.
2. Pour on the soured milk and treacle.
3. Grease two loaf tins and line them with crushed rye then spoon in the dough.
4. Bake, without proving, in the bottom half of the oven at 175°C for about 2 hours.

COOK'S/BAKER'S COMMENT
An easy bread that "looks after itself", which can be a great help in times of kitchen crisis.

Index of recipes

Picture credits

Page 6 Watercolour drawing by Carl August Ehrensvärd, "*Skåne girls hay-making.*" Photo by Nationalmuseum, Stockholm.
Pages 8–9 Drawing by Åke Arenhill.
Page 13 Watercolour by Nils Månsson Mandelgren. Folklivsarkivet, Lund.
Page 14 Two photographs. Folklivsarkivet, Lund.
Page 15 Watercolour by Frans Lindberg. Kulturen, Lund.
Page 17 Silhouette. Nordic Museum Picture Agency, Stockholm.
Pages 18 and 19 Easter letter. Kulturen, Lund.
Page 20 Painted wall hanging. Private collection.
Pages 20–21 Drawing by Åke Arenhill.
Page 22 Watercolour by Frans Lindberg. Kulturen, Lund.
Page 23 Photo by Gunnar Lundh. Malmö Museums.
Page 25 Painting by Bengt Nordenberg, "*Tithe Meeting in Skåne.*" Photo by Nationalmuseum, Stockholm.
Pages 28–29 Watercolour by Frans Lindberg. Kulturen, Lund.
Page 29 Photo. Offerlinds Spettkaksbageri, Genarp.
Page 42 Drawing by Åke Arenhill.
Page 47 Photo. The Stiernberg Collection. Kulturen, Lund.
Page 48 Photo. The Stiernberg Collection. Kulturen, Lund.
Page 49 Photo. Folklivsarkivet, Lund.
Page 51 Drawing by Åke Arenhill.
Pages 52, 53 Labels. Vin- och Sprithistoriska Museet, Stockholm.
Page 54 Song books. Lennart Kjellgren.
Page 55. Photo. Nordic Museum Picture Agency, Stockholm.
Page 56 Private collection.
Page 84 Photo by Peter P. Lundh. Höganäs Museum.
Page 90 Painting by J. W. Wallander, *Threshing Rape. Skåne.* Nordic Museum Picture Agency, Stockholm.
Page 91 Photo. Folklivsarkivet, Lund.
Page 92. Photo by Bebbe Ohm. Malmö Museums.
Page 93 Two photos. Folklivsarkivet, Lund.
Page 95 B/w photo. Folklivsarkivet, Lund.
Page 98 Photo. Folklivsarkivet, Lund.
Page 99 Watercolour by Kilian Zoll, *Harvest Home Celebration in Skåne.*
Page 100 Drawing by Åke Arenhill.
Page 101 Two photos by Peter P. Lundh. Höganäs Museum.
Page 103 IBL Bildbyrå AB, Ljungbyhed
Page 104 Photo. Folklivsarkivet, Lund.
Page 105 Watercolour by Nils Månsson Mandelgren. Folklivsarkivet, Lund.
Page 106 Photo. Folklivsarkivet, Lund.
Page 107 Photo by Gunnar Lundh. Malmö Museums.
Page 108 Music programme. Private collection.
Page 109 Sydsvenska Dagbladet 1939.
Page 110 Sydsvenska Dagbladet 1939.
Page 110 Two photos by Gunnar Lundh. Malmö Museums.
Page 111 Sydsvenska Dagbladet 1939.
Page 111 Photo by Gunnar Lundh. Malmö Museums.
Pages 124–125 Section of Öresund navigation chart. ©Swedish Maritime Administration permit no. 0105138.
Pages 124–125 Flag pin. Private collection.
Page 126 Sydsvenska Dagbladet 1939.
Page 126 Photo by Gunnar Lundh. Malmö Museums.
Page 127 Photo by Gunnar Lundh. Malmö Museums.
Page 128 Photo by Gunnar Lundh. Malmö Museums.
Page 129 Photo by Gunnar Lundh. Malmö Museums.
Page 129 Menu and watercolour of the Malmöhus. Malmö Museum Archives.
Page 132 Watercolour by Nils Månsson Mandelgren. Folklivsarkivet, Lund.
Page 146 Photo by Peter P. Lundh. Höganäs Museum.
Page 147 Photo by Per Stiernberg. Private collection.
Page 149 Photo by Olle Berggren.
Page 150 Photo by Gunnar Lundh. Malmö Museums.
Page 152 Bookmark. Private collection.
Pages 162–163. Drawings. Nordic Museum Picture Agency, Stockholm.
Page 165 Photo by Olle Bogren.